D1614743

Life is a Cucumber

BY THE SAME AUTHOR

To Sea in a Sieve
Bulls in the Meadows
I Know the Face, But ...
Not on your Telly!
I Say, Look Here!
It Isn't all Greek to Me
Bear With Me

PETER BULL

Life is a Cucumber

Some not frightfully 'Belles Lettres'

'Life is a cucumber. One minute it's in your hand and the next minute it's up your arse.'
(Old Arab Proverb, adopted by the Greeks)

PETER DAVIES : LONDON

Peter Davies Limited
15 Queen Street, Mayfair, London, W1X 8BE
LONDON MELBOURNE TORONTO
JOHANNESBURG AUCKLAND

First published 1973

432 01954 5

Printed in Great Britain by
Northumberland Press Limited
Gateshead

Quite simply, for Don Lawrence Busby

Line drawings by Keith Lavender

The author would like to thank *Variety* for their kind permission to reproduce both his letter regarding the run of *Pickwick* and Mr David Merrick's reply; also *The Village Voice* for their permission to quote the extract from an article by Mr Ken Sobol.

Contents

Foreword

EVERY now and again I come across a slim volume, usually well-bound and expensive, entitled *Belles Lettres.* Within are a series of reminiscences and poetry, which I suspect have been reposing in the author's drawer for many a long year. 'Beautiful Letters' is the direct translation of this type of miscellany, but of these specimens are not always included. Yet I've admired the phrase for some time and longed to achieve the completion of such a tome.

The trouble with an occasional writer is that there comes a time when his Muse is sulking and unwilling to give a hand to an undedicated and uninventive vassal. I was never so conscious of this as when the 'I' flew off my typewriter.

There I was, seated comfortably at my desk, tossing off something for Woman's Hour about My Kindergarten Reunion and in 'one foul sweep' (as my dear mother used to say) I was rendered helpless. I must explain that I cannot write in longhand legibly enough to satisfy the average reader. This is a result of having learned to print my letters at the aforesaid establishment of learning and I've never bothered to join them up since the age of nine.

Anyhow I hied me to the typewriter firm who usually service my machine, and the gentleman there expressed his astonishment at what had occurred. I asked him why.

'Oh,' he replied, 'with most of our customers it's the "e" which flies off first. Then the "a". The "i" comes a bad third.' There was a pause and he asked,

'Do you write about yourself much?'

I found myself blushing all the way back on a number 11 bus as I ruminated on the incident. I had not realized to what extent I had relied hitherto on this particular letter. It is true that every book I have written has been largely autobiographical, apart from the Bear Book, and even that was instigated by my own experience, or rather that of my Teddy. It was clear by the time I got back to my bereft desk that my egocentricity has brought things to a pretty pass.

Incidentally the 'I' has flown off twice since, presumably because it wasn't mended properly, but cynics, and indeed I, in one of my rare humble moods, would say it was A Warning Sign. But what to do and how to stop myself from over-using the fatal letter? I suppose I could have a special typewriter constructed which would exclude it in the capital form. But then everything I wrote (I mean i wrote) would look like *archy and mehitabel* or e.e. cummings which would confuse readers and wouldn't fit in with my style at all. And what pray would happen if I wanted to make some serious pronunciamento about Italy or India to say nothing of Islington and/or Iver (the place) and Ivor Novello (the actor-playwright and composer)?

Another alternative would be to ration the number of 'i's' to be used on any one page. A bell would ring and a slight electric shock would strike my two hands. Then presumably there would be a spate of phrases like 'me had a bath' or 'heave away handsomely' which would tend to exasperate and bewilder the gentle reader and eventually render him violent. Oh dear, how worrying it all is! If only it had been the 'q' which had fallen off. I could have managed very comfortably without that and when it came time to mention the monarch, I could have referred to Her Majesty and everyone would have understood.

Foreword

After a great deal of reflection I decided that the Warning Sign had meant I was not to embark on any more autobiographies. And that's fine by me, and would be even finer if I could think of anything else to write. I suppose it might be considered a little precious if I started calling myself Peter Bull in books and using the 'I' as a totally different person who was observing my actions, like Mr Boswell vis-à-vis that Doctor Johnson. Well, not really, I suppose, but that sort of thing.

I recall being deeply impressed by Dame Agatha Christie when, in *The Murder of Roger Ackroyd*, the narrator turned out to be the murderer. Perhaps I could repeat this formula and kill myself off too. That really would be a case of killing two 'I's' off with one stone wouldn't it.

Apart from the occasional article, I have kept my writing trap shut for two years, when I abandoned a third re-write of what was intended to be my final autobiography. It simply wasn't working, as my best friends (and I use the phrase wholly sincerely) didn't hesitate to tell me.

But buried among the debris there were bits which I liked and from other sources I gathered stuff which amused me in other media and I thought just worth salvaging. So here it all is. No umbrage either way I hope. 'Belles Lettres' they aren't.

I

LIFE IS A CUCUMBER IN GREECE

1. *Life is a Cucumber*

MR YPSILOS is an exceptionally tall Greek with huge feet, who once sold me some land on the island of Paxos in the Ionian Sea. The other day he came huffing and puffing up the hill leading to my little house, carrying a big bag of plums. Automatically the phrase 'Beware of Greeks bearing gifts' crossed my mind, but before I could marshal any defensive action, he had deposited himself in a fairly upright deck-chair and started to get his wind back.

After dishing out a plum or two, he offered me the rocky piece of land just behind my property for ten million drachmas, roughly a hundred and forty thousand pounds. I was absolutely flabbergasted, but preserving my cool, I said:

'Oh, but Mr Ypsilos, how kind of you to think of me, and how very cheap!' At least that's what I thought I'd said. But unfortunately I'd used the Greek word for 'expensive' instead of the one for 'cheap'. But in a country where the word for 'nothing' also means 'anything', it is easy to get confused.

Mr Ypsilos stared at me for a moment or two, took out a pencil and a scruffy piece of paper, made some calculations and then announced that he'd made a 'lathos' (mistake) and he had *MEANT* one million drachmas. In spite of this sudden drop in price, I gently but firmly declined his offer, and thought it was the wrong moment to remind him that I had bought the original piece of land on which To Spiti Mou (My House) stands, for forty pounds. Not, I fancy, that he has ever needed reminding.

After a few minutes of complete silence, he got up and shuffled off. I knew I was probably safe from another business visit for the year, but it is the sort of incident which makes living in Greece so stimulating and endearing. The fact that the luscious looking plums brought intense suffering in their wake, due to their unripeness, caused only a minor ripple in my love affair with the Greek way of life.

Last year in Corfu, while discussing something disagreeable which had happened to him, Costas, a shoemaker friend of mine, informed me that Life was a Cucumber. As I am a wizard at recognizing Greek words denoting food, I was able to translate the phrase immediately without understanding what it meant. Costas looked quizzically at his companion, who averted her eyes from him with an embarrassed smile, and explained that life was like that vegetable in that it was sometimes bitter, sometimes sweet, and varied in appearance and content. Later I learned from him the true and phallic translation. Arab in origin but now spread over the whole of the Middle East, to say nothing of the title page of this book.

I have added this phrase to my repertoire to join such old-established favourites as 'Scassehi' (Shut Up!), 'Na Xerathees' (Dry Up!), 'Etsi-Ketsi' (Dodgy) and 'Po-Po-Po-Po-Po' (Oh goodness me!) and now feel fully equipped to meet any situation. I have also more or less mastered those Greek gestures which mean so much. The extraordinary shrugs of the shoulders, and the looks heavenwards which, accompanied by a curious clicking noise, express disagreement or disbelief.

But to boast that now 'I'm one of them' would be lunacy. I don't think that I will ever understand them and I'm certain that they feel exactly the same about me. This year I found myself cleaning out my oven because Alekkos, my factotum, had omitted to do same. I found myself getting into a rage about the things left undone which should have been done, until I realized that, if he had cleaned out my oven, and someone had caught him at it, it would have meant 'loss of virility'. The same with plate-washing or any of the chores that some of us British gentlemen are so good at.

It's like the Return of Hospitality problem which I experience on the island. I am now sufficiently accepted among the islanders to be included in most of the festivities, like christenings, marriages and funerals. You may think I am being flippant, but sometimes the last are the jolliest of all, and certainly one is spared the agony of watching the bride in new but torturing shoes, having to dance by tradition with every man present. The funeral bakemeats are very handsome, and if the deceased is of a great age, the rejoicing is natural and respectful.

Anyhow, I discovered quite early on that no-one would come up to my house for an actual meal. Sometimes, if passing on their way to fish, they would drop in and grudgingly accept an Ouzo. Usually all they wanted was a glass of water. I then discovered that Greeks must always be the hosts, and I also noticed that they don't like, or pretend not to like receiving presents. They sometimes hardly acknowledge them, and if they are given to the wives, the husbands will never refer to them. Yet, years later, one realizes that they've registered, like the Peter Jones table mats of Street Scenes of London, which were on the wall of some Greek friends of mine, disguised as pictures.

So there was only one solution in my mind. I decided to give an End of Term party, and ask everyone I could think of. In the early days Alekkos used to look at my list and say it would never do to ask Christos if Stephanos was coming. They hadn't spoken to each other for ten years. At first I deferred to his verdict, but as the years steam by I get bolder and bolder and last year I had a major triumph when two protagonists in a current court case sat next to each other the whole evening, and seemed to settle several of their differences there and then.

The first party was pretty nerve-racking. At Alekkos's suggestion I had put the time around 7 to 7.30 in the evening and we were ready for them at that hour. I had not of course made allowances for Greek time which is at least two hours behind Spanish time, and you all know what *that* does to your schedule. By nine o'clock my house guest and I, both fortified and ruined by a great many Ouzos, were about to put the bowls of taramosalata away in the fridge, when we heard the sound of singing coming up the hill and a few minutes later most of the village came through the gate in high fettle. A fair percentage of them had brought gifts and one of the problems every year is how to get rid of the many bottles of Koum-Kouat, which is the usual offering on this sort of occasion.

Anyway, they were, if not under my roof, at least on my land, and the evening seemed to go with a swing. It was mainly masculine and the few wives and sisters who came sat demurely, spreading huge portions of tara, etc. on great chunks of bread.

In fact the tara went so well that the next year we decided to have more of the stuff. However, I thought that those long biscuity things called Gristicks would make an innovation and everyone could dip in at will. The usual procession came up the hill with their bottles of Koum-Kouat or Ouzo, and sat down on the four seats, three beds, six lilos and Greek carpets provided, and gradually I brought out the food. Masses of Gristicks decorated the tables and, to encourage the others, my English friends and I dipped deeply and lusciously into the tara. No-one followed our example. Finally I asked Mitsos, the captain of the ferry-boat, why no-one was eating.

'Poo einai to psomee?' (Where is the bread?) he yelled in a voice of thunder. Luckily I had half a dozen loaves tucked away in case of emergency. After that the tara disappeared at a rate of knots. Sometimes the hosts don't get a chance to sample the goods, as in the case of the six kilos of sausages and the huge birthday cake we'd brought from Corfu with 'Kalo Chimona, Lakka' (Happy Winter, Lakka) written on it in icing.

It's a phrase (Happy Winter) which they use a great deal when one is leaving the island, but one cannot help feeling that it is said in a wistful way. Winters out there can be pretty bleak, with the rain pouring down for weeks on end, and the ferry-boat to Corfu constantly unable to make it, with a resultant shortage of stores. All the young men go off to sail away in 'sips' as they call them and the old people wonder, as in England, if they'll see another spring. Until I visited the Mediterranean climes during the war, I was entirely convinced that they were all sunny Winter Paradises. Not a bit of it. Owing to the stone floors, lack of adequate heating and general dampness, I maintain that it is far healthier, and on the whole warmer, in our much abused country.

But the Greeks don't grumble (much), and it is this acceptance of their fate which has made them so enormously endearing to anyone who gets to know them. It is really hopeless for a Greek-born American lady to come back to her birthplace and start banging on about her washing machine. They simply listen to her as if it was a fairy tale. Our café-cum-post-office-cum-cinema introduced a television set the other day. It lasted five days. Only the young people gawped. The older generation missed their games of 'Tavli' (a sort of Greek backgammon) and Spiro did no business with his drinks and sweet cakes, so back the hideous machine went to the shop.

It is unwise of my otherwise intelligent English neighbour to think that it would be a good idea to teach the Greek ladies cookery. I told her that I thought she would end up like poor Irene Pappas in '*Zorba*' stoned to death by the men of the village, who like their plates always to be cold, and likewise most of the supposedly hot food. They are immensely stubborn about taking advice, even on the rare occasions when they ask for it. For years I've been giving it to the proprietor of a hotel in Corfu, who seems genuinely to want to know why the hotel next door does so much better. I try to help, suggesting that the customers would rather not risk death every time they go to swim and nearly slip through the broken slats on the jetty. It would help even more if he would put the name of the hotel up somewhere so that everyone could see it and not think that *his* establishment was the annexe to the 'Mega'.

He listens in a sort of disinterested way and I can see the dreaded sign in his eyes that he is already dreaming of adding another floor to his establishment, which will make him at any rate *higher* than next door, even if he never fills the rooms.

But as he is the gentleman who once asked me if I thought it would be a good idea to put up a sign in the restaurant saying 'The customer is always wrong' it is difficult to reason with him. I pointed out that dreary people might not see the joke. After my explaining the meaning of 'dreary' he announced: 'But I don't want dreary people. I only want jokesey people like you!'

You can't win with the Greek, which is one of the reasons why I didn't feel remotely boulversé to Mr Ypsilos' direct frontal attack about his land. I have been haggling with him ever since I first came to the island nearly ten years ago. We have maintained a bizarre love-hate relationship, realizing that both of us possess what the other wants, in his case the driving force being money, in mine privacy. Since my original purchase I've been obliged to buy a little more land every year at vastly increased prices. Fair enough under the circumstances, until he started a sort of blackmail by bringing prospective customers to view the land directly alongside mine.

The only way I could deal with these intrusions was to put on an alarming performance for strangers in the hope of deterring them from entering into negotiation with Mr

Ypsilos. This took the form of joining whatever guest(s) I had in residence at the time in a series of erotic dances, accompanied by three radios, going full blast on different stations. At various moments we would stop our gyrations and hurl abuse and/or rocks at each other. Whether this ploy was successful or not I don't know, but by the end of the summer I was so unnerved that I made an offer for the remainder of the little plateau on which To Spiti Mou stands. Mr Ypsilos countered with an astronomical figure. Nikos Kaloudis, my adviser and guardian angel, and I split the difference and I've never regretted the purchase.

One might have thought that Mr Ypsilos would have left it at that but not a bit of it. He still thinks I have inexhaustible funds and want to turn Lakka into a sort of Very South Kensington. He is certain that I want to be surrounded by my English friends. Any visitor who arrives by ferryboat without warning is alarmed by this tall old man wrenching their luggage out of their hands and attempting to guide them up the cliff in order to sell them a bit of the land just behind mine. He simply can't or won't understand that this is the one thing I have come here to avoid. Truth to tell, the phrase 'away from it all' has no meaning for the average Greek.

Certainly, on the island of Paxos almost everyone is related. The possibility of wanting or even being able to get away from relatives and friends wouldn't occur to them. I once asked a Lakkiot now living in London, George Argyros, who on the beach at that time was *not* his cousin. He looked around him and eventually said, pointing at a pretty girl, 'She isn't.' There followed a long pause as he surveyed the rest of the bathers, then, 'He isn't. At least I don't think so.'

A few months ago I attended the marriage of Andreas Apergis and Calliope Apergis. The fact that they had the same surname even before their marriage didn't surprise me in the least. Around Lakka there are really only four main families, Aronis, Mastoras, Argyros and Apergis. This makes marrying locally outside the family almost an impossible event.

It was a very moving ceremony for me as I knew the full story of the bridegroom's background. He is one of the nephews and adopted sons of Alekkos Apergis, who had looked after me and To Spiti Mou ever since I set foot on Paxos. A family man himself, he had a beloved brother who died in the saddest circumstances during the war.

Paxos was under Italian domination at the time and the people were deprived, almost to starvation point, of food. Always dependent on Corfu or the mainland for supplies, they had been cut off at the sources by their so-called conquerors. The only asset the islanders had was their incomparable olive-oil. The Italians confiscated a large percentage but, by guile, the Paxiots were able to conceal some in the caves, which lie just outside Lakka and are nearly a mile and a half in depth. Oil barrels were lowered over the cliff and stored until they could be taken to the mainland near Parga to be exchanged for wheat, chickens and, if possible, meat. The young men of the village formed a rota for this hazardous journey, which was naturally carried out at night and when there was little or no moon. It fell to the lot of Alekkos and his brother to take their turn and they reached the mainland without incident, and were able to complete their bargaining. Just as they were about to push off, a shot rang out and killed the brother instantly. The enemy had obviously been alerted.

Alone and terrified, Alekkos rowed back to Paxos (a distance of some fifteen miles) with his dead brother in the stern of the boat. The horror of the journey can be imagined but there was more agony to follow. As he drew near the shore he could make out the figures of all his relatives and friends on the beach. They were very excited and happy. It appeared that his brother's wife had just been delivered of a son.

The infant was christened but not long afterwards the mother died and Alekkos took him over, in addition to the two boys already in his care, sons of his second brother who had also died suddenly. Andreas, one of the two, was the bridegroom on this occasion and Yanni, his senior, is our barber, a profession he doubles with running a smart new café owned by yet another, elder, brother. A real family business this café, for with Yanni are his wife and his wife's father, Diogenes. Goodness these relationships! Yanni's wedding I had attended several years earlier and this time I felt more able to converse and make some sort of contribution to the gathering.

I was touched by the unity of the Apergis family and Alekkos's pride in his very handsome nephew. He has never talked to me about his tragedy, but the signs of it are sometimes mirrored in his face, and there was something about his early manner towards me, which is now totally explicable.

Anyway, there was nothing to mar the gaiety that Sunday night. The bridegroom's party was assembling at Alekkos's lovely cool house. I decided to walk, though, if I'd known that Ho Pappas was arriving by taxi, I would have cadged a lift. Ho Pappas is our chain-smoking priest who is much beloved by the village, though he is not my idea of a Holy Man, even if he did bless my house for the equivalent of seventy-five new p. That included a great whoosh of Holy Water in the direction of the loo. He was a ferry-boat captain at one time and no-one has been able to explain to me his violent change in professions, though by the time he'd taken up his clerical appointment, he'd acquired a wife and at least one son, a penchant for duty-free cigarettes and comfortable travel—as on this occasion when there was no question of sparing expense.

It took me about twenty minutes on foot and I got there hot and sweaty, to find Andreas still dressing for his own wedding. He had an exquisite new suit, probably purchased in Athens when on leave from his merchant 'sip'. (The Greeks cannot manage 'sh' or 'ch'. Shelagh Delaney's daughter Charlotte was constantly referred to by the

Kaloudis family as 'Salad', a name we all still stick to.) Anyhow, the bridegroom seemed completely composed. Looking back on it, I now realize that I have never seen a wedding couple as fully in command of the situation as Andreas and Calliope; I suppose it's all part of their upbringing and sense of security. For even in the case of the three orphaned children, they have been cushioned by the love of Alekkos and his family ever since.

You may have read somewhere that there are hardly any psychiatrists in Greece, and it is easy to understand why. Practically all the children I know are so well adjusted that one seldom if ever hears a grizzle or a whine. They also appear frightfully self-contained and will sit quietly for hours without bothering their parents. Their stamina is fantastic and when I left the wedding at a little past midnight I saw a little tot aged four, still beating his hands in time to the music with the greatest energy. And he wasn't the youngest there (and awake) by any means.

Alekkos came out to greet me, bringing a tie as I told him I didn't think I possessed one in my wardrobe. There had been a bit of confusion on the previous day. I had asked him to lend me a 'cravati' which turned out to mean a bed. I should have said 'gravata' which only shows how 'etsiketsi' the whole thing is. Alekkos was looking very smart indeed, and, giving me a sharpish look, called Mrs Alekkos and suggested she should give my shoes a bit of a polish. I tried to stop her doing it herself but it was useless. Meanwhile, numerous nieces were bustling around with children and making them look beautiful. There were sweetmeats and Ouzo in profusion and a general air of excitement and festivity.

Suddenly there was a grinding of brakes and one of the island's four taxis disgorged Ho Pappas and his son's girl friend. It was a curious duo but, like most of his actions, didn't seem to surprise anyone in the least. He took off his high round hat and the usual ridge of white on his forehead was as striking as ever. He and I are old friends (and I do hope my grounds for this belief aren't entirely founded on Messrs Benson and Hedges) but the mysterious thing about him on this particular evening (it was at six o'clock we assembled) was that he'd brought none of his props with him. Alekkos produced these one by one from inside *his* house. There was the three-hundred-year-old Bible, belonging to the church, the censer and the candlesticks. While we drank, Alekkos was searching for two candles of roughly the same size but finally had to settle for two wildly dissimilar ones. 'Then berazi' (It doesn't matter) said Ho Pappas on his third Ouzo, which after 'Avrio' and 'Meth avrio' (tomorrow and the day after tomorrow) is the most used phrase in the Greek language.

The next arrival at the house was the 'koumbaros' (godfather), who wasn't an Apergis for a change. He was a Mastoras and there is a village on the island called Mastoratika where most of the people bearing that name live, which must present a problem or three to the postman. A Greek godfather takes his part extremely seriously and during the wedding of his charge, his role is the most important, apart of course from the priest and the bridal couple. Kyrios Mastoras was accompanied by a young man who bore the tulle bouquets, to which were later attached lighted candles, which were to be carried by the happy couple throughout the service. The godfather himself held on to the pearl chaplets, which are worn from half-way through the service and form an integral part of the ceremony; they are joined to each other and are in the shape of wreaths.

About six-thirty the bridegroom asked, shouldn't we all be going, so we started on the half mile walk to the bride's house. No-one in our village ever seems to think that it would be a good idea to get married in an actual church and I must say that the private home is a good deal cosier as a choice. But the procession to Calliope's house was fairly unconventional (to me) with its atmosphere of a picnic about it. We kept on crossing the paths of other guests, who chatted the bridegroom up along the way. Most of us were carrying our presents with us. Mine was a fairly awful coffee-set which I'd managed to buy in Lakka at close on midnight the evening before. I hadn't realized till that moment in the main Café Neon that it was customary for the bride and bridegroom to have their gifts on display after the wedding. I asked Spiro Café's pretty wife to help me. There had been a great rush on household gifts that week so I was happy to see that there was only one other set of coffee-cups among the presents. I couldn't however see a single farting-horn, which used always to form part of the bride's trousseau. How it worked must be left to your imagination.

All day long the 'Maestro' had been blowing in from the sea and my flowers had taken quite a beating but here in the centre of the island it was comparatively tranquil and the place they had chosen for the actual ceremony was a narrow passage between a wall and two houses joined together.

When we arrived the bride's relatives and friends were all ranged on chairs and she herself was there to welcome us all. Then it was a question of finding the best position from which to watch the proceedings. A kind friend beckoned me to a high place by the wall, which was almost as good a piece of standing room as that nabbed by Panagioti, the official photographer, who was gently mocked by the guests throughout; they swore that every shot he took would turn out 'mavro' (black). Just before the service began, I saw a lady arrive on a donkey and hurriedly change her shoes and join the audience, after tying her transport to a nearby olive tree.

This is exactly what my good neighbour, Mrs Good, does when she comes to the annual shindig at To Spiti Mou, though she doesn't arrive on a donkey. She usually comes by sea as she lives on the next headland to me. She built her handsome villa largely single-handed. Blessed with almost perfect Greek (she worked for NATO on the mainland for many years) she had been observed shortly after dawn, for months on end, in her boat *Polyxenia* towing small barges full of cement, sand, etc., to unload on the beach below her proposed house.

We live in a harmonious and totally unclaustrophobic relationship and I couldn't ask for a more helpful neighbour, though she shames me by her industry. Kyria Kalee (Mrs Good to you, in Greek) keeps bees, milks goats who've been unwise enough to stray into her garden, grows rare and exotic flowers and veg, entertains countless relatives and friends throughout the summer, cooks superb meals, brushes scorpions nonchalantly away from her front door and somehow finds time to give English lessons for free to the young people of Lakka.

Ho Pappas put on some white vestments and we were off. He stood on one side of a table and the happy couple on the other. Alekkos lit the candles and I got nervous that a sudden gust of wind might catch the bouquets which the bride and bridegroom were holding close to them. But all went smoothly and the chanting was shared by the priest and a younger assistant. The only snag for them was that a large percentage of the congregation gave a running commentary to the kiddiwinks and those who couldn't see most of what was going on. Ho Pappas dished out some sharpish looks to a splinter group of guests who sat at the far end of the garden, drinking and smoking and paying absolutely no attention to anything.

Suddenly in the middle of a long harangue by Ho Pappas there was a huge laugh. It was explained to me by my friend the harbour master, standing near. Apparently during the ceremony there comes a phrase about the bride having to 'fear' her mate (obviously the equivalent of our now old-fashioned 'obey'). In Greece it is the cue for the bride to stamp her foot on that of her groom and on this occasion she did it so realistically that her almost husband let out a yell. One of the other village customs is that the bride has the names of her unmarried girl friends on the soles of her wedding shoes and the first one that is rubbed off is that of the one who is going to be married next. Judging by the amount of dancing the bride has to do later, I would have thought that not only all the names, but most of the shoes would disappear on the same day!

For me, the high point of a Greek wedding is when the two joined chaplets are placed on the couple's heads and changed round several times. The service ends with a kind of Holy Communion and wine is drunk three times by the bride and then the censer is swung by Ho Pappas in all directions to bless us all. Then the pair go round and round the table, while they are pelted with rice and sugared almonds. Ho Pappas gives warning before the ceremony against the throwing of the latter because of the black eyes and worse sustained by happy couples. Not of course so happy at the loss of an eye which occurred on one occasion. The godfather at the Apergis nuptials was constantly darting behind the bride to cut the danger risk.

Having successfully survived this ordeal Andreas and Calliope plus the principal actors and immediate relatives take up their positions (seated) to receive the congratulations of the guests. This is the only part of the ceremony which is remotely reminiscent of its English counterpart, because I didn't catch a glimpse of a picture hat in uptown Lakka. While we filed past, Ouzo and Koum-Kouat were being poured into glasses. The latter, to which I have briefly referred, is an Ionian speciality, a liqueur made out of bitter-sweet Corfu midget oranges. Excessively saccharine, it's not much use to an old diabetic like me and I don't quite know what to do with the many bottles that kind guests have brought me in the last few years. No-one seems ever to drink the stuff except at weddings and funerals, but it is popularly supposed that it would make a nice present to take home. There is a green variation (it's usually a repellent bright orange) which isn't so sweet and someone told me that it was 'not half bad' when used in conjunction with Greek brandy, but I can't pretend to endorse this verdict.

Anyhow there were plenty of sweetmeats and glasses of

beautiful water to wash it down with on this occasion, and the dancing was beginning. The leading musician at these affairs is blind but he plays a number of instruments expertly and can be heard teaching the bride's younger brother the accordion at rather too frequent intervals. The bride, by the way, is the daughter of Stephanos, who keeps the café on the jetty and serves the most nutty and honeyed baklava in town. He and his wife had organized the wedding feast superbly and there was never a hitch, even though one hundred and twenty persons turned up, instead of the ninety who had been invited.

The dancing was lively and of great variety. The Greek folk numbers were interspersed with variations of the 'twist' and, rather surprisingly, the tango. Gradually nearer the house, the Wise Virgins, including the writer, had established their positions favourably for the food, and suddenly their zeal was rewarded. Pastitso was placed in front of us and huge portions there were of this favourite Ionian dish, composed of macaroni and meat, covered with a brown batter. I managed to keep my hands off my portion as I thought there must be some form of 'starter's orders' in the shape of Grace, but certain customers simply couldn't wait and they were tucking in like maniacs. Eventually Ho Pappas was given a nudge and realized it was up to him, so he got to his feet, blessed the food, and, I think, the universe. A dear unknown lady opposite wished me 'kali orexi' (good appetite) and we were off. She never took her eyes off me or my plate, and ordered second helpings for me as if she were the hostess and I'd just been undergoing a long fast.

The second course was the ox that Kyria Good had reported seeing that morning being hauled up the hill, and very tender it was in a thick rich sauce, with potatoes to match. I usually have to stew all the meat I buy in the village, as it is always so fresh and hacked about, and curiously enough you pay as much for bones as you do for steak. Cool water-melon completed the meal and after that we sat back replete and happy, glasses kept continuously at the ready for toasts.

A very old man with a wicked moustache made a short speech wishing health and happiness to the bridal couple. I understood most of it, particularly when he mentioned that he was a hunter of birds, and I realized he was the man from whom I duck during the 'trigonia' shooting season. These are the turtle doves, which are a great culinary delicacy. During their migratory visits to the island, practically every male dusts off his gun (which is sealed by the police for the rest of the year) and takes a pot shot at them. I remember a series of bullets ricochetting past the house the first year I was in residence. My guest at the time seemed a trifle disturbed but I assured him (from under the table on the terrace) that it was the customary way of welcoming newcomers to the island. The shooting season is mercifully brief but very noisy.

Wicked Moustache appears to have the monopoly (for shooting purposes) of Mr Ypsilos' land just behind my house and makes the fullest and most dangerous use of it. He was much safer making a speech which he did quickly, and apparently wittily, for he sat down to considerable applause and laughter. A lull followed until, quite spontaneously, four or five ladies down my end of the table started singing a wistful but melodious song. After a few lines the men took it up, and from then on they sang alternate verses. It was, I was told, a song about marriage which has been passed on down the generations and ends with the pious hope that all boys and girls would find the same happiness as the current couple.

Soon it was back to dancing and there was some pretty spectacular stuff, now that the wine had really begun to circulate. There was bottle, glass and table balancing, culminating in our butcher doing his stuff. He is a huge man who dances superbly and, if sufficiently encouraged, will do his speciality. This involves him lying on the ground, arching his stomach and inviting all and sundry to step on it or even jump on it. I declined as I didn't want to spoil either (a) a beautiful friendship or (b) the choice of lamb chops if and when they arrived.

I left a little after midnight and Alekkos accompanied me to a fairly negotiable road through a maze of olive groves and small cliffs of rock. I had been thanked by the hosts, the bride and bridegroom, for coming.

'It is we who thank you,' they always say, and I walked down the hill and up the one to To Spiti Mou. I thought a lot about the evening's events. I had been told so often about the marriages of convenience and how many Greek men will marry a girl for her dowry and/or olive trees, or because her father will provide a good job. There are also the shot-gun weddings, which occur frequently, or even worse the shot-gun non-weddings, when the family discover that a man has had sex with an unmarried daughter, and it is traditionally up to them to force him to marry her. If he refuses it is quite customary for the father or one of the brothers to kill the man and in Greece this particular crime is condoned to the extent of meting out only a couple of years or so as sentence for the killer.

Andreas and Calliope are a beautiful couple, and judging by the glances and handholding at Alekkos's name-day party the previous Sunday, a marriage of convenience it wasn't.

2. *Anglo-Greek Way of Life*

OUR one Greek doctor lives several hours' mule ride from my house and normally pays us a weekly visit, on Wednesdays. It's not always easy to fall ill on Wednesday. He arrives by the ferry-boat with the bread as he appears to have no transport of his own.

Once I had a young American staying with me who was seized by a mysterious malady. It took the form of violent nausea and giddiness every few hours and complete normality between attacks. Fortunately it seemed to start on a Tuesday, so I was able to shanghai the doctor on the following day on his weekly visit. He diagnosed sunstroke and instructed my chum to lie quiet and drink plenty of liquid. Easy instructions and the invalid settled down to a maddening jig-saw by Jackson Pollock, accompanied by extreme constipation. I had one or two mild laxatives handy which I shovelled down his throat without result.

Then headaches of a fearsome kind started, and he was by now unable to keep anything down, so I decided to send for the doctor again. At that moment violent storms rent the island, and the ferry-boats, all transport and the telephone system were rendered immobile. The bus was 'arrostos' (ill) and even the path down to the village was dicey, being several inches deep in water, and pitfalls were endless. By the time I started on my journey, my friend had turned his face to the wall and appeared to have given up. Later he told me that there came a moment when he was completely devoid of self-pity and was just feeling sorry for me having to explain to his parents that their son had died of constipation on a Greek island.

I sloshed my way down to Spiro's café, the usual hub of what village activity there is. The only occupant on this occasion was an English-speaking native, who related a droll story about how a friend of his had died of constipation only the year before, after no movement of the bowels for nine days. As my chum was on his eighth I did not feel encouraged.

I sat gloomily eating yoghourt in the café until Spiro Petrou arrived. In the village we all regard him as a worker of substantial miracles. He manages somehow to run the telephone exchange, the post-office, work from 5.30 in the morning till nearly midnight, never lose his temper and always listen courteously to the maddening questions of foreigners and inhabitants alike. On his arrival I mimed what was the matter with my house guest, not a frightfully attractive exhibition, but it was enough for Spiro. He summoned from nowhere a young motor-cyclist who was dispatched to find the doctor. An hour later he reappeared, soaked to the skin, with one very large pill, manufactured I suspect for consumption by a horse. The medical adviser was too busy with patients at his surgery to come himself. He sent his kindest regards.

I bustled up the hill with the pill, to find my poor friend in a sort of coma. I gave it to him, and he swallowed it with difficulty, only to regurgitate it in its entirety later. I discovered subsequently that he should have chewed the bloody thing. The next morning he was worse and I was desperate. I practically swam down the path and in tears begged Spiro to help again.

This time he rustled up a lorry complete with driver, and

we set off for the doctor, whom we found attending to a queue of about thirty sufferers. He couldn't leave, so I gave a repeat performance of my diagnosis of my chum's complaint, which held the largish audience enthralled; I added a fresh touch by imitating a douche. Had the doctor got one I asked in mime, making squirting noises up my posterior? He watched fascinated, and then confessed that *he* hadn't such a thing but there might be one, he thought, in the toy shop in the capital.

Off we went in the lorry, and shortly I was in the store. I gave my usual performance and the very gloomy old proprietor disappeared up a ladder and brought down a lovely old enamel container, with rubber tubing attached. I was studying it in a slightly mystified fashion when an elderly lady snatched it out of my hands and demonstrated its use. Graphically, as a matter of fact. I found out, through an interpreter, that she was a retired but trained nurse. I grabbed her joyfully and half an hour later we were in To Spiti Mou. She, soapy water and the machine, wrought an immediate miracle, and my hard-done-by friend, assisted by willing hands, proceeded to the flushing loo at a spanking pace.

All's well that ends well, whatever that means. I might add that, since the acquisition of my richly equipped medicine chest, no-one has even had a cold in my building except for my own dear medical adviser (British version) who sprained his ankle. Goodness, how sad!

But one's sense of proportion seems to be all at sea when living for a great deal of the year in completely alien surroundings. It's like the sense of time which descends on one, only 24 hours after reaching Greece. One might easily have been there for 24 days or 24 minutes. It probably has something to do with the seeming lack of any kind of pressure or sense of urgency, which permeates the atmosphere. In many continental countries 'manãna' is one of the most used of local words but the Greeks go one better with 'meth avrio' (the day *after* tomorrow). And I do know that one of the most frequent sounds you hear in the cafés at night is an argument between people about what day of the week it is.

I'm certainly totally different to my Chelsea self out in the Ionian islands and all my reflexes undergo violent change. Who for instance would have ever believed that the day would come when I would judge my friends almost entirely on the amount of water they use? It's a shaming thing to admit but I think I ought to come clean. I have to rely on winter rain-water to supply me with enough to get me through four months of summer. I do have a shower and a flushing loo, but I also have a garden which is very thirsty indeed, being mainly constructed of cement and fairly peculiar compost.

As a result frightfully hygienic guests aren't all that welcome unless they can be turned into slatternly sluts and bums within minutes of their arrival. The ideal guest is the one who says, 'Oh, I don't want a shower. I prefer the sea every time. I *love* the salt to stay on my skin.' Then there are the dreamboats who think it's frightfully healthy to use the woods as a loo. These two types are unfortunately rare birds and so are the ones who never want to wash their clothes, though the water consumed in this operation is re-usable on some of the hardier plants. Don't you believe that detergents are death to all things in the garden. My cactuses would even welcome Brown Windsor soup.

Practically every ounce of liquid can serve a double function though there is still an area of doubt about the water in which eggs have been boiled. It certainly can't be used for making the tea as I've found out to some of my guests' cost. The results are disgusting and there is an old wives' tale that washing with it brings one out in warts. After preliminary experiments with the leaves of the fig tree, I have surreptitiously given it to some of the healthier guests and studied their complexions for a few days afterwards. Not a blemish!

A good deal of finger-wagging has to go on about the use

of the lavatory. The plug is not to be pulled unless deemed absolutely essential and some guests are so frightened by the written instructions about not putting paper down the bowl, etc., that they get constipation (I now have endless remedies for *that*) or take to the hills. Sooner or later of course it will probably be perfectly economical to install one of these conversion jobs, you know the ones I mean, which cheerfully turn sea into fresh water, but until that happy day there'll always be a problem.

One of the more bizarre operations you can witness on a stormy night is the sight of me and any guest unlucky enough to be in the offing and awake, girding up our loins to cope with any incoming and blessed rain. Every known receptacle is carried out into the open air, the water tank lids are removed and the biggest basin is placed under the hole in the canvas awning to catch the water.

But the real excitement, for me at any rate, lies in the possibility of the rain being continuous and forceful enough to soak through the tiles on the roof sufficiently to reach the gutters and so into the main water tank. Unfortunately this is rarely achieved and the success of the operation requires four hours' continuous driving rain, a rare occurrence in this land of violent but short-lived storms. If it is achieved, a ritual Dance of Rain is performed on my tiny dance floor by the cliff edge. Guests may join in at their own discretion.

Those fortunate enough to survive the soaking and the damp house will reap their reward the next day, when they will be allowed to centralize all the droppings from heaven and wash themselves and their clothes to their hearts' content as long as the garden can enjoy the repellent dregs.

Although I have emphasized the curious feeling of time suspended in a Greek island, it is astonishing how quickly something can be done if the mood is on the inhabitants, like indeed supplying lobsters or refrigerators. Ah, that surprised you! You wouldn't think we'd indulge in luxury articles like that would you? After electricity had reached our isle, it seemed expedient to change from gas, but, cad that I am, I didn't really think that the new facilities would function as satisfactorily as they have proved. I hung on to my old gas-Electrolux like grim death. It was a bit temperamental but, as you probably know, you can just turn it upside-down from time to time, give it a sharp bang, and it will continue to give you loyal service. But chance and terrible snobbery combined to make me change my way of iced life.

I'd been over in Corfu and just as I was leaving the swinging Calypso Hotel, I was told I was wanted on the phone by a Mr Harrison. It so happens that I know several Mr Harrisons and I was surprised and flattered when it turned out to be Mr Rex H. He was on a yacht apparently at Paleocastritsa on the West Coast of Corfu, and had every intention of coming over to Paxos on the following day, if I was likely to be in. I would be in, I said; and that was that.

Arriving home I stuffed every soft drink I could find into my tiny old fridge and made as much ice as I could muster. The next morning I found that it had packed up. At ten o'clock I marched down to the village and into the local friendly grocers. He had hardly anything edible for sale but he did have several large beautiful refrigerators. I chose one and said I'd pay cash, if it could be at my house within the hour. Well, you've never seen anything like it. By eleven it had been installed and considering it is at least half a mile up a steep hill through a path beset with thickets, it was a remarkable achievement. The fact that the old gas number suddenly started working on its rival's appearance was just macabre, particularly as it exploded shortly afterwards, but without causing loss of life.

Around one o'clock, a huge yacht arrived at the harbour entrance, and I made violent signals to Rex about berthing. However, the ship chose to anchor where she was, which seemed lunatic to me as there was a tiny swell running and great gusts can spring up from nowhere. I beetled down the hill and got one of the harbour experts to row me out to the yacht. But apparently the French skipper of the big ship (hired) wouldn't budge, though we assured all concerned it was perfectly safe to come further into the little port. No dice. And eventually Rex came ashore in the launch with the Leslie Bricusses. Leslie who wrote and composed *Doctor Dolittle* was also responsible for getting me into that film, about which far too much anon.

Anyhow they made the hill without difficulty and enjoyed the first fruits of my new refrigerator. It does happen to be called 'Pitsos' (trade name) and I did make the error of announcing to various villagers that I had an 'oraios megalos kenourios putsos' which apparently meant that I had a beautiful new big cock, which wasn't quite what I'd intended to communicate, though goodness how lovely if it had turned out to be true. After a short time we adjourned to the yacht whose lounge was about three times the size of my poor little Spiti. In the middle of lunch I suggested we were drifting on to the rocks at a rate of knots. Rex was fairly alarmed and had to go and inform the captain, who then upped anchor and I had just time to finish the 'afters' before they sailed off.

I am not jealous of people who own yachts. I always think it a bit sad that they are so completely at the mercy of the captain and crew who can persuade them how essential it is to get fresh water, oil, petrol, spares and go to the port of *their* choice. It seems to me that they might just as well be running an old-time slave ship for the amount of freedom the guests enjoy. Mind you, it's all made to look like home with real flowers and real copies of *Vogue*, to say nothing of the duty-free liquor and cigarettes. But, for some of these folk, going ashore becomes an ordeal, because it involves an immediate loss of security, for it is only on board that they can enjoy a sado-masochistic relationship without danger.

It is only on their own ship that they feel they can

order their champagne cocktails and martinis with impunity. Directly they walk off the boat they are *sure* that they are going to be swindled port, starboard and midships. Worst of all they have to face the fact that they are in a foreign country and they might have to talk to the *peasants*, my dear; and although it can be amusing sometimes, isn't it odd they don't seem to understand a *word* we are saying? And of course the visitors speak their English loud and clear. Once I heard a gentleman in ever such a smart yachting cap yelling at my Local Friendly Grocer:

'MY WIFE WILL BE ALONG IN A MINUTE,' as if *that* would help mutual understanding.

On the other hand, if you decide to stay on the boat, there is little hope of peace and quiet. The engineer is usually charging his batteries, which rules out any question of a siesta, as the rattling of generators is more disturbing than the giant turbines at sea. In any case the younger members of the group have probably decided to go water-skiing directly after lunch and soon the sky will be rent by the most hideous of all noises abroad, that of the cultured British voice raised in excitement.

'Can't you go a bit faster, old chap?' etc.

It is fortunately a law in some Greek ports and bays that no-one is allowed to make any sort of noise during siesta hours, and in Corfu town the public aren't even allowed to applaud a particularly brilliant stroke during one of the extraordinary cricket matches which take place in that delightful city, survivals from the British protectorate. By the way, in a recent match the visitors were surprised to find three new faces in the Home Team after lunch. The Captain explained that three of his players had been taken ill. The Corfiots won the day, and it was believed in many circles that the newcomers, who saved the match, had been released from prison specially for a few hours.

If I'm disturbed during siesta time, I shake my fist at the offenders, and throw a few bad potatoes at them, and I imagine they refer to me as 'that dotty old man on the hill' and go back to reading 'Jennifer's Diary' on board their ship.

I found during the war, when I had a small landing ship under my command with seventy men on board, that it was claustrophobic to a worrying degree. But at least it was during times of National Emergency. With a big yacht it needs very careful selective acumen to arrange the right combination of guests. I know one particularly ruthless owner who said in front of them:

'We're getting rid of these on Saturday and having a fresh lot flown out.'

A lot of yachting people never seem to go ashore at all and therefore never taste the delights of foreign cuisine. They are perfectly happy to open their Fortnum and Mason tins and have exactly the same type of food as they would have for the remainder of the year. The result of all this is that the natives resent their presence in their harbour as they never spend money ashore and probably even get their mooring free.

I except from this ridiculous tirade certain types of yachtsmen and shiphandlers for whom I feel nothing but respect, even if I can't share their enthusiasm. I refer to the gents who actually propel their own boats, like Sir Alec Rose, and who know all about helms, winds, spinnakers and main boom guys.

Sailing under your own command can obviously be the greatest fun if you can go where and when it suits you. Usually you have your family or very close friends to crew and you can curse and swear at them as much as you like. I knew one small yacht-owner who quite seriously made his wife salute him every time he stepped aboard the poop deck. And she *loved* it.

On this type of craft there is a competitive spirit, and binoculars and/or telescopes are kept at the ready to compare the merits, measurements and tonnage of any other similar vessels in the vicinity. There is a sort of Who's Who of Yachts (or should it be a What's What of Yachts?) which is consulted avidly. But on the whole the skipper-owner of the small yacht is an admirable bloke, adventurous, good-tempered and with a natural instinct for the sea and the smelling out of the most secluded anchorages.

I meet them all the time in Lakka and the other day as I was swimming across the bay a voice said:

'What a ripping little spot you've found. Come aboard for a snifter.' It was the sort of language that I expected to find only between the covers of a novel by Mr P. G. Wodehouse or the late Ian Hay. Not a bit of it! The speaker was for real, over eighty years of age and still captaining his own boat. His only crew was an extremely pretty girl of some twenty summers (and absolutely no winters) totally unrelated, and apparently obtained quite simply by advertising in the Personal Columns of *The Times.*

Casual accosting from a passing yacht is infinitely preferable to me than the sudden arrival of the unexpected guest with the happy smile on his, her or their face, which freezes the moment they see the look of horror on mine. Although the postal, telegraph and phone service to Lakka is a trifle erratic there are ways of warning one of an approach but it is a constant surprise to me how conceited the mildest people must be to imagine that their popping up like jacks in the boxes would be welcome at any time of night and day.

I loathe being taken at a disadvantage, particularly when I am the host in such a hospitable country as Greece. But I am not exaggerating when I say that people seem to drop in far more frequently to Lakka than to the swinging King's Road, Chelsea, London, S.W.3, England. Acquaintances I have met perhaps twice briefly in my life appear out of nowhere with beautiful matching luggage expecting a Capriesque villa or, at worst, the Paxos Hilton. I remember hearing a wealthy Italian lady describing To Spiti Mou to some friends:

'Peter has such an amusing leetle house. But he has no staff.' It was the way she said 'Staff' which killed me. There's hardly room for me, one friend, two wardrobes and a loo, let alone a sleeping-in butler and three footmen. Except under exceptional circs, I usually dispatch the sudden visitor(s) to the room above Mr Mouse's restaurant where the pong of fish and the loud playing of bazouki records through the night are a guarantee that they will scamper off to Athens at crack of dawn the following day.

In any case the accommodation problem on our island is considerable at the best of times because anyone wanting to let rooms or whole houses won't ever make known their availability until the last moment, so convinced are they that a rich American, Dutch or Italian family will come along and want to check in for the whole season. The result is that, even with guests who *are* welcome, it is sometimes a question of sending them to the capital where there are more amenities, although the transport situation tends to become a tidge 'etsi-ketsi'.

Sometimes the situation is so desperate that it becomes ridiculous and therefore jokey, as on the occasion when Nikos Kaloudis brought over a caique-load of Albert Finney and a few friends. Since we already had six people to lunch that day, it was just the twenty-two who sat down or stood, I having opened every tin in the building. Dinner that evening was something else. The menu consisted of Larry the Lamb and they'd brought *him* with them. The only snag was that 'Salad' (Charlotte) Delaney noticed his living absence while she was in fact eating one of his more tender portions. A resourceful young American called Neal Noorlag took her on his knee (she was four at the time) and spun an ingenious tale about how Larry the Lamb had come to Paxos to stay a bit with his Dad, where he was working in the fields. Thus was a nasty scene averted.

But it must be admitted that in this paradise the variety of food leaves something to be desired. On the other hand it is an undoubted fact that everything tastes much nicer (a) in fine weather, (b) when you eat it out of doors and (c) if you have been in the sea exercising every known muscle for hours. I find that if I open a lot of tins of meat cooked in olive oil, mix a few fresh veg with them, go berserk with the garlic, dowse the whole thing in wine, then my guests mistake me for the Galloping Gourmet or old Mother Craddock and tend to fall down on their knees in ecstasy.

Everyone in England says to me, 'Oh but you must have such lovely fish.' On the contrary one must not have such lovely fish. I see half the population go out in the early morning and, when I see them later in the day and question them, they look sadly and say 'Teepota' which, amusingly means 'Nothing' or 'Anything'. If it means 'Anything', in this case you may be sure that Anything is going whizzing down their own stomachs and not into the shops. And why not for goodness sake? They caught the bloody things. On the rare occasions when a proper 'catch' comes in, the whole operation assumes a Top Secret aura and you hear whispers of 'psaria' (fish) from all corners of the village. People come out of doorways as if the Pied Piper were calling them and disappear in roughly the same direction, but hardly ever to the harbour.

The fish, such as they are, will eventually be traced to some very unlikely place, like the tailor's shop or the barber's. By the time you've located them there is only one red dogfish left and everyone else is walking around with smug expressions and small bundles under their arm. The reason for comparative absence of fish in our immediate area is believed to be that the waters were severely depleted during the war, when a state of near starvation necessitated dynamiting the sea for food. This of course jeopardized the supply of young fish and I imagine that, even among the sub-marine world, there is some sort of bush telegraph warning the denizens of danger zones. Anyhow I have been informed that it takes a minimum of 20 to 30 years to build up a decent fishing harvest again. One macabre aspect of the dynamiting business is that you see a great many one-armed Greeks who have had bad luck while attempting to feed their families. These days a pretty hefty prison sentence awaits the offender, but I'm told from reliable sources that dynamiting still goes on everywhere and I would have to sleep like the dead not to hear evidence of it just below To Spiti Mou.

Luckily I don't care enough about fish to take violent steps to obtain it but I know that if I bruited it abroad that I was in the market for some big stuff, it would arrive somehow at my door and not for once be transported to be sold to one of the swankier hotels in Corfu.

Take the case of the Birthday Lobster. Barry Justice was staying with me and I thought I'd give him a treat on his natal day. The usual 'keftedes' (meat balls) seemed hardly adequate for the occasion. Now one of the mysteries to me of modern civilization is the fact that a lobster costs a king's ransom anywhere in the world. There seems to be no rhyme or reason for the price to be exactly the same in a city miles away from the sea as it is in a remotish place, where they appear to be plucked from the ocean like seaweed by Those Who Know.

I thought it was unlikely that I'd be able to lay my claws on one this particular day but at least I'd have a try. I popped down to the village early and made some enquiries. Everyone shook their heads or rather nodded them, with a clicking noise to express their total disbelief in the possible success of my quest.

Three hours later I was on the far side of the bay—having made my daily pilgrimage across—lying on my face and minding my own business, which on this occasion was an attempt to even my tan, partic under the chin(s), this necessitating some pretty bizarre positions, I don't mind telling you. Suddenly I was conscious of a hissing in my ear and, turning over, I observed Nikolaus Apergis of the smallest Café Neon in Lakka, who appeared to have arrived from the other side of the bay in a dinghy with a small totally unexplained child, not his certainly. He informed me (putting on an early Warner Brothers spy face) that there was Something waiting for me in a bag on his mule outside the schoolhouse and would I get into his boat please?

His request upset my usual health routine, as I always swim back to the other side but I felt I couldn't refuse as he was treating the whole thing as a hush-hush operation which must be carried out with the utmost delicacy. Ten minutes later I was looking at the largest lobster I'd ever seen. Except that it was a crayfish (they don't seem to grow claws in Greece to become lobsters, but what the hell!).

It was poking its dear enormous head out of a bag on the side of Nikolaus's mule and looked irresistible. Barry and I were obviously in for an orgy and, whatever the price, it was impossible to draw back now.

Nikolaus preceded us (the child and me) up the hill with his precious burden still twitching in the bag. I scurried up afterwards, anxious that the birthday house-guest shouldn't be too alarmed by the odd cavalcade. I reached To Spiti Mou just in time to see the two gents chasing the crayfish, which was careering across the property at a rate of knots.

They eventually caught it and Nikolaus tied it up by the claws. Mr Justice, who was already drooling at the mouth but unfortunately not in Greek, asked me what the hell we were going to cook it in. I pointed out a few largish saucepans to Nikolaus who 'po-po-po-po-po-poed' them. I said I'd go down to the village to see if I could borrow some adequate receptacle at once, as he insisted that the beast must be cooked while it was still alive, in order to taste its best. My house-guest made some reference to the RSPCA, which didn't help at all and Nikolaus and I beetled down the hill. The child had disappeared earlier down to the village to Tell All as was obvious from the air of expectancy when I entered the hardware-cum-postcard shop. Half Lakka seemed to have assembled there.

I selected the largest saucepan in the building, and took it along to my Local Friendly Grocer, who was deep in conclave with Nikolaus. I put the object on my head which was good for a laugh but not, in the opinion of the bystanders, good enough to cook the beast in. We stood around perplexed until my nice L.F.G. produced an absolutely new petrol tin, with no petrol in it, and it was generally agreed that, with the top removed by a sharp instrument, it would suit our purpose admirably. I removed the saucepan from my head and returned it to Hardware who didn't seem to mind a hoot.

Armed with my prize, I got back up the hill to find the resident Chef, Birthday Boy himself, eyeing the captive with a mixture of pity and lust which was alarming to view. He grabbed the tin out of my hand and with little clucking noises, such as you make to soothe a crying baby, enticed the ferocious beast inside it. Then he filled it with water, set it on the stove and brought it slowly, humanely, to the boil. I say humanely because he assured me that this was the correct procedure, since the lobster is first gently warmed to sleep and apparently remains unconscious while being boiled to death. A likely story!

A few hours later we were plunged into the most gorgeous meal I can remember. I don't think one *can* have too much lobster, or in this case crayfish. The phrase 'Enough is as good as a feast' is simply not true as far as I am concerned. 'Slightly more than enough is as good as a feast' is how I would amend it. The next day, after, it must be admitted, a pretty sleepless night, I took the claws and a bottle of wine down to Nikolaus as a present for having brought about the orgy. I then hied me to the grocer, who, I'd discovered, was really responsible for supplying the actual creature and paid 'to logarismo' (the bill). It was just short of four pounds, monstrous but worth every drachma.

I shall probably repeat the whole performance another year but at the moment it's hell's own job trying to get the shops to stock anything original. No-one makes stuffed vine leaves or taramousellata or any of the really Greek hors d'oeuvres. Every annual party I invite all the grocers in the hope that they will be more enterprising. Last year two of them seemed deep in appreciative consumption of some white beans I'd bought in tins in the capital. This year I went to both of their emporia and found myself facing a mountain of the damned stuff. I had to buy a great many and, throughout the season, out of guilt, I've had to go on with the bloody things. Their original pride when they showed them to me is rapidly changing to shame, as no-one in the village seems to fancy them but me. Mainly, I suspect, because the rogues are charging more than they do in the capital for them.

But it'll be a long time before they stock kippers and peanut butter, which a shop in Corfu does. Though for sheer originality I would like to draw your attention to the hunchback greengrocer in our capital, who amazingly displayed a small basket between his cucumbers and green beans, which contained prophylactics. But any town that sells enemas in its toy shop soon loses its capacity to surprise.

And although there's not much chance of our ever being able to breed our own lobsters or even crayfish, at least an attempt is being made to grow a few veg on the arid property. During Don's first visit to Paxos he surveyed the barren waste which formed my garden and said, 'What we need is a good compost heap.'

'Yes, Don Lawrence,' I said meekly (for that was his name in those days. His stage name. He's really called Busby like the soldiers' furry hats.) I was frightfully impressed by this pronunciamento and was then given my instructions, which were to put every scrap of food left on plates or discarded from culinary purposes into a pit he dug near the edge of the cliff.

This went on for many days and didn't smell all that nasty because he covered it with sifted earth from time to time. So I went happily and usefully about my business until I saw The Rat. I said to the Head Gardener, 'Look here, Don Lawrence, there is a rat eating our compost.' I thought it best to break it to him bluntly without any ranagazoo. He gave me a sharpish look and asked if I had a copy of Laurence Durrell's *Prospero's Cell* handy. I said yes I had. He took a cursory look at the end of the volume and pointed to the Appendix for Travellers. I followed his finger and read 'An excellent rat poison is made by pounding the centre of asphodel bulbs and mixing with a little ordinary cheese'.

He gave a snort of triumph, disappeared into the undergrowth and came back with a large bulb-like thing resembling an onion, which he proceeded to hack about mercilessly. Melding some cheese into the remains he put the whole Asphodel Rarebit on to a plate which he placed at the edge of the compost heap. The rat had by now popped off for its siesta, but I'm here to tell you that we never saw it or the Chef's Own Rat Dish again that year.

I was frightfully impressed by the whole thing and the next year, when I was on my own, I tried it out all over again when another rat made an appearance. Of course it may have been the same one. Hadn't thought of that. How worrying! The point is I hadn't realized how poisonous the heart of an asphodel can be. It's all very well for Messrs Fowler in their *Pocket Oxford Dic.* to describe it as an 'Immortal Flower in Elysium' when it burns the bejesus out of you if you start hacking it up. After I'd mashed it with some lovely hard feta cheese, I found myself in excruciating agony and couldn't believe that the rat was likely to endure half of what I was suffering.

I put the dreadful dish down with my bandaged hands near the compost heap and awaited results. I never saw the rat again but I did glimpse a huge white cat who seemed not only mad about compost but also Asphodel Surprise.

Since then we've tried all sorts of experiments. I can't pretend that the compost heap was remotely successful. A few tomato plants, beans and melons started to grow out of it but never reached puberty. We put new seeds in it but they dreaded it obviously and never surfaced. We even tried to make an outside loo into a lovely vegetable garden, having read somewhere about the Japanese producing things of great beauty from land fertilized by human excrement. I kept falling into the vast pit Don had dug which didn't make for Harmony in the Home.

The next compost heap seemed harder than the ordinary earth so we've abandoned that line of approach. However last year we had some extraordinary luck in our guests. Owing to pressure of business Don and I had to take separate holidays out there and it wasn't until the end of the summer that I got out to Greece again. The weather was bizarre in the extreme and the natives kept on saying that there had been nothing like it for a hundred years. You know how they go on and on and on saying that sort of thing. For once I did believe them. Because you don't expect four cloudy days and heavy rain to pour down in August around the Mediterranean but this is exactly what happened.

Hell for the tourists but heaven for To Spiti Mou. Unlimited showers for guests, flowers and me for a change. Chris Mason, a friend of ours and an exceptional Jack of All Trades, achieved in three days what we'd asked Alekkos to arrange to have done during the last three years. Chris constructed steps to the shower, an avenue of baby cypresses, mended the roof, pruned the olive trees and was able, because of the dampness of the earth, to make a bed or two in which the tougher vegetables might survive.

Then a delightful American couple, called Mary and Ted Taylor, took over the house after we left. They had arrived in Lakka in the late spring and had slept on the beach most of the summer. They had met first in Vietnam, married and wandered round Europe, earning enough in the winter to spend long carefree summers in the sun. Although they weren't remotely waif-like, the Greeks had adopted them as their own and treated them with great tenderness and generosity. I found that they had been inside far more private houses as guests in a few months than I'd done in eight years or so.

They loved To Spiti Mou and during the autumn seem to have worked like beavers. The last pictures they sent, taken just before they left for America, show an enclosed vegetable garden with a wall round it and what looks like rich earth contained therein. They had been given cuttings from friends in the village and we can't wait to see what sort of rich harvest will emerge.

I just hope that the shoes I had perforce to leave in the last compost heap haven't fructified, if you know what I mean.

3. *Thought for Food*

THE other day some ass brought a ghastly book to Paxos. It was called *The Diet Book for Diet Haters* and it just about ruined my holiday. It's difficult enough to get *any* food on the remote island without having to count up how many grammes of carbohydrate you are consuming. I gather that the diet suggested in this tiny tome is sweeping America but is in fact founded on one suggested a century ago by an English gent called William Banting. Well anyhow that's the one good thing which *does* come out of it. I've always wondered where the phrase 'I'm banting' came from and now I know.

It has a nice old-fashioned ring about it, though it must have been a bit confusing in the old days when somebody actually said 'I'm banting' to the diet inventor himself, who presumably replied rather angrily, 'No, *I'm* Banting.' It might even have led to fisticuffs. Old Banting weighed fourteen stone, which sounds sylph-like to little me but he was only five feet five inches in height. He was a coffin-maker by profession which would be enough, I imagine, to make anyone a tidge cautious. In 1864, the Banter, by now light and not so heavy, wrote a treatise with the wildly attractive title of *Letter on Corpulence*.

He had apparently lost forty-six pounds in a year by eliminating sugars and starches from his daily intake (so what else is new?). He stated that (and I quote) 'the great charm and comfort of the system' was that its effects were palpable within a week of trial. Apparently carbohydrates produce the pyruvic acid which one stores in one's system. To tell you the honest truth I have never heard the word 'pyruvic' in all my 'puff' (naval term meaning 'life'), but I do see that it's a jolly good word to use in 'Scrabble' as it uses up that tiresome 'v' in a droll way and will infuriate one's opponent. Here, half a mo! I've just looked in the *Pocket Oxford Dic.* and can find no trace of 'pyruvic' or for that matter 'puff'. So where does that leave one? Full of carbohydrates and an imaginary acid (as far as the Fowler Brothers are concerned).

Which is the reverse of what happened to dear Mr Banting, who was enabled 'to look and feel like a human being' (and I quote again) having got the now nameless acid out of his system, just by eliminating sugars and starches from his diet. He was however allowed or allowed himself meat, fish, sea-food, fowl, eggs, cheese and FAT. I put the last named in Caps because it astounded me so. But in this repulsive book I have been studying, it says in black and white that 'a high fat diet actually helps you to lose weight'. It goes on at length on the subject and in such a way as to put you off your food for many a long day, with sentences like 'By eating large quantities of fat, you set in motion a process which stimulates the pituitary gland and thus burns your body fat at a higher rate.'

I suddenly see myself at a chic restaurant and asking for 'large quantities of fat, please' and watching the reaction of other guests, to say nothing of that of the waiter who has been unwise enough to ask me what I want.

The greater part of the book is devoted to the number of grammes of carbohydrates each article of food contains and as I'm only allowed sixty grammes of the bloody things a day, I do see that the consumption of a dehydrated apple or three isn't likely to reduce weight, as each contains just the four hundred and thirteen grammes. On the other hand I can apparently go berserk over canned anchovies, steamed bass, butterfish (whatever they are), eels (ugh), garlic (goody, goody!), goose, chopped mint, oxo cubes, roast partridge, pheasant, pigeon and pigs' feet.

Mr Derek Manley, who wrote the volume, was not, I think, catering for a patient living in a fairly remote Greek Island, because I've never clapped eyes on a pig there, let alone its dear little tootsies. In fact most of the things Mr Manley is so keen on me eating are totally unavailable on Paxos. Perhaps I would be better off with Mr Banting's basic diet. I do see 'large quantities of fat' at the Greek butchers, whenever I visit their emporia, but not a sign of a pheasant or partridge. And I've managed to keep away from making any sort of jape about grouse. So far!

Perhaps because Mr Manley says I can have as much champagne, vodka, gin, whisky and brandy as I like, to say nothing of wine, it's just a disguise for the Drinking Man's Diet, about which everyone has been banging on for so many years. I've never paid much attention to it because I don't happen to be a Drinking Man. It's not that I am ashamed of the fact or proud of it. It just so happens that I class myself as an Eating Man and as far as I know there isn't such a thing as an Eating Man's Diet. If only there was, I wouldn't run the risk, as I now do, of turning into an alcoholic if I can't get hold of some geese and/or eels. Soon I may be reduced to drinking some 1972 Bovril, laced up to the hilt with vodka.

It must be admitted that Mr Manley comes straight to the point with the disconcerting question 'What about snacks?' What *about* them indeed? I thought they'd be death to the weight-reducer but he appears not to mind. In fact he gives the go-ahead signal, though his choice seems a trifle arbitrary. It appears that I can eat as much Roquefort cheese or pâté de foie gras as I like. There is also no limit on the number of permissible frankfurters. But, greedy as I am, they are unlikely dishes to tempt me at eleven o'clock in the morning, even if the Messrs Fortnum and Mason had been kind enough to open a branch in downtown Lakka. However I do read that I can stuff myself silly with hard-boiled eggs, though we all know that over-consumption of these can bring its own problems.

Maddeningly Mr Manley says nothing about yoghourt, which everyone tells me *must* be frightfully good for me, and of which there is an unlimited supply on sale in the village. I have a sneaking feeling that he wouldn't entirely approve of the five heaped spoonfuls of peach jam which I pop on top to take away the slightly sour taste. Ah! Heaped! The very word suggests quantity.

The next question Mr M. asks me is a much easier one to deal with. 'How can I stop the temptation of reaching for a chocolate or a sweet?' My answer to that is to make sure that there *aren't* any chocolates or sweets in the building, let alone cakes, biscuits and bread. Well, franchement, I think this is a fearfully selfish way of entertaining one's friends who are apt to be as thin as wraiths and yet much addicted to the eating of bread, etc., partic. the etc. If Mr Manley thinks I'm going into a monastic retreat to get me through this traumatic period, he's got another think coming.

The only sensible and cheerful pronunciamento which he makes in the entire book is his reply to 'Would it help if I had only two meals a day?' To my huge relief and delight he announces 'Skipping a meal will hurt rather than help.' Thank you, Mr Manley, for those few kind words.

While on the subject of food (and, truth to tell, I am rarely off it) the other day I received an invitation to a Dinner Party. Even the phrase seemed to me as old-fashioned as 'Cocktail Party' and, to confuse me more, printed in the corner of the card was 'formal'. I couldn't think what that meant, as most of the invites I get these days are of the 'Come as you are, I doubt if there'll be anything to eat. You know what Camilla is like' variety. So I was in a quandary as I didn't know what the form (to say nothing of the Formal) was.

So I went out and purchased for a modest sum two volumes which looked as if they might assist me. One was *Manners for Men* by Mrs Humphrey ('Madge of *Truth*' it says in brackets) and the other *Etiquette for Gentlemen, a Guide to the Observances of Good Society*. Although I don't think either tome was published in the last year or so, they proved full of sound advice for those of us who Don't Go Out Very Much. And if you want to share the information I have gleaned from it, you are more than welcome.

Got your pencils and paper? Then stand by to copy it all out before you return this book to the library. Are you sitting comfortably? Then I'll begin.

'An invitation to Dinner denotes a greater mark of esteem and cordiality than is conveyed by an invitation to any other social gathering. Many a young man feels nervous about his first dinner party. He wonders if he should wear gloves, taking them off at the dinner table. Let me set his mind at rest' (says Mrs Humphrey). 'He need not wear gloves. In fact *he must not*.'

I thanked heaven for this first admonishment because I really couldn't bring out my woollen mitts through which the forefinger of one hand and the thumb of the other come brazenly through. It might easily have led to my being dropped by Decent Society, into whose ranks I seemed to have been admitted. Possibly, it would seem, by error.

'When he is shown into the drawing room he at once goes up to his hostess and will then be told what lady he is to take down to dinner and be introduced to her. Here is his first difficulty. To converse with a perfect stranger is always one of the initial social accomplishments to be learned and it needs practice. Ninety men out of a hundred offer a remark upon the weather; but unless there has been something very extraordinary going on in the meteorological line, it is better to avoid this subject, if possible. A girl at Ascot said to me, ("Madge of *Truth*" not Me!) "That's the eighth man who has informed me that it's a beautiful day." Up came the ninth with the very same observation and both she and I felt inclined to titter like schoolgirls.

'"Do you know everybody here?" is a good beginning and this leads perhaps to the acquisition of some information as to the other guests. At table there will be more to suggest Topics. The Floral Decorations often lead up to conversation. The *colours* remind one of pictures and the lady on one's right may be asked if she has been to any exhibitions. Does she paint? Has she read the novel of the hour? Does she bike? At this rate our novice gets on swimmingly and may be safely left to himself.

'At the dinner table the first thing to be done on sitting down is to unfold the napkin and place it across the knee. The menu is then consulted and a mental note is made of any favourite dish so that it may not be refused. (Some notes on that curious language known as "Menu French" will be found on another page.) But all this time a flow of small talk must be kept up with one's partner though, however hungry one may be, the viands must not be chosen as a topic for either praise or blame.

'Eat slowly, noiselessly and with your mouth shut.' With your mouth shut. (Are you *mad*, Mrs Humphrey? Or can I call you Madge?) 'In dealing with bread use neither knife or fork. There is a story of an absent-minded prelate, who with the remark "My bread, I think" dug his fork into the white hand of a lady who sat beside him.' (Perhaps in that case you *should* wear gloves. Cancel Madge's and my last instructions on this subject.) Although the lady from *Truth* with truth adds 'He had been badly brought up or he would not have used his fork and the white hand would have experienced nothing worse than a sudden grasp.'

'One word before we start on the soup. It requires some expertness and practice for a man with a moustache to take soup in a perfectly inoffensive manner. The accomplishment is worth some trouble. Be very sure not to make any noise when taking soup. By now some wine will have been poured into your glass and it would be wise to remember two things. Do not empty the glass in one gulp—it is very vulgar. And do not forget to wipe your lips *before* drinking *and* after. The sight of a person who neglects this precaution is not pleasant.

'Soup is never helped twice nor is fish. If a servant in error asks "Any more soup, sir?" you *must* reply in the negative. A shake of the head will suffice. The meat course should offer no difficulty unless peas are provided. These must be gently pushed on to the fork and so conveyed to the mouth.'

Oh, Madge, how you mistrust us weak mortals. Did you honestly think we were going to resort to the knife as a method of conveyance for our peas?

'When slices from a joint, game or poultry are handed round, the vegetables, gravies and sauces accompanying them are handed after. It is usual to wait for these etceteras. For instance no-one would commence upon a slice of roast beef or mutton without potatoes or gravy, nor upon a piece of pheasant without browned breadcrumbs, or bread sauce or gravy. I say "no-one" would do it, but I have seen it done, whether in absence of mind or from pressure of appetite I cannot pretend to say. It is a mistake however.

'Vegetables are *always* eaten with a fork and it is out of fashion to lift asparagus off the plate in the fingers: the newer and better mode is to break all the edible part off with the fork and so convey it to the mouth. Globe artichokes give only a very small feast. Raise the leaves on the fork and gently press with the teeth to obtain the flesh and juice, removing the leaves by the end of the fork. It is difficult to do this comfortably and many decline the struggle for so small a return.'

Madge is adamant about the eating of fruit and there are no half measures about her way to handle grapes.

'Grapes are taken up singly and afterwards the skin and

seeds have to be expelled as unobtrusively as possible. It is a matter of great difficulty to accomplish this by any other method than using the hand. The forefinger is curved above the mouth in a manner which serves to conceal the ejectment and the skin and seeds are in this way conveyed to the plate.

'Nuts must be cracked with the implement provided, and it behoves all who eat them to make as little litter as possible. Eat slowly, noiselessly and don't pause or hold long arguments and forget that the dinner is being kept waiting by you. Use your napkin before taking up your glass and when you put it back on the table. Also use it *immediately* after you have taken soup.

'At the conclusion of each course, place your knife and fork side by side on your plate. If you cross them it is taken as a sign that you desire a second helping, and such ought never to be requested at a formal dinner.' (Well, Mrs Humphrey, in *that* case I may not go to this here party.) But hold on, what is coming next?

'Liqueurs are handed round at dessert and there is generally a choice such as "Chartreuse or Benedictine, Sir?" to which it is unnecessary to reply "*both* please" as a historic young man did once.

'When the ladies rise to leave the dining-room, the gentleman nearest the door opens it for them and stands beside it until they have all passed through, when he closes it. However anxious he may be to join them in the drawing-room, he must not do so until the others make a move. Sometimes if he is very or rather "out of it" when politics or sport are under discussion, his host says to him, "I'm afraid you are bored. If you would like to join the ladies, don't stand on ceremony." But on the other hand he may dread the ordeal of entering the drawing-room alone, and feel that the safer way is to wait for a convoy.

'The ordinary rule is that the gentlemen join the ladies all together, the man of highest position leaving the dining-room first, the host last. Tea is then carried round in the drawing-room, and the gentlemen take the empty cups from the ladies and put them in some safe place. Should any lady sing or play, the gentleman nearest to her escorts her to the piano and helps her to arrange her music, to dispose of her gloves, fan, handkerchief, etc.' (Where *can* he put her etc.?)

'If this is not possible, "listening in" to a wireless concert will follow if time permits, but if the dinner has been enjoyable, conversation will have prolonged it until well past nine. A bright genial host and a lady who has charm make the time pass very quickly, and pleasant conversation for half an hour or so brings ten o'clock round, when the guests take their leave.

'It is scarcely etiquette for a young man to leave first after a dinner-party. But should a young man have an engagement of a pressing kind, such as a promise to escort ladies to a ball, he must withdraw in good time, explaining the position to his hostess.

'In the country the host usually makes it his business to see his lady guests to their motors. In town he sees that this is done by his servants.' But, Madge dear, what about *me*? How do I get from the front door to my omnibus without a breach of etiquette? Why can't one of the ladies give me a lift in one of *their* motors?

However, thanks to your instructions, I think I shall survive this formal Dinner Party to which I have been bidden, but what's this, Mrs Humphrey? You say 'it would be *unpardonable* to appear in thick walking-boots or shoes; and the necessity for immaculately polished foot gear has cost the young man of the present day many a cab. His varnished shoes must show no trace of mud or dust. To tell the truth, he often carries a silk handkerchief in his pocket wherewith to obliterate the traces of the latter. The pocket-handkerchief used with evening-dress must be of white cambric, and of as good colour as one's washerwoman will permit. It ought to be of fine quality. The hair must be short and very well-brushed.

'It used to be the custom to tip the servants on leaving the house where one has dined as a guest but this has fallen into disuse. The custom of giving shillings or half-crowns to the servants no longer reigns: though there are always good-natured folk who will not let it absolutely die out.'

That's torn it, Mrs Humphrey. I *am* good-natured but I haven't got a shilling or a half-crown to my name. I shall tear up the invitation and go off in my thick walking-boots and long hair to Alf's Diner in Shepherd's Bush where they don't serve grapes or asparagus and I can blow on my soup like a steam engine.

II

LIFE IS A CUCUMBER IN ENGLAND

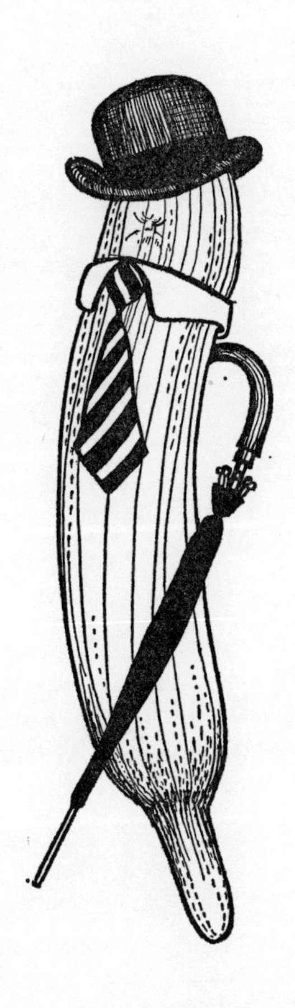

4. *Egos and Alter Dittos*

It's curious how devastating an effect can be caused by an innocent remark, if it is badly timed. How often have *you* been furious when someone has said: 'How well you're looking,' when you are in fact feeling ghastly or recovering from a hangover. The reverse is also true. 'You look a bit pale. Are you sure you're all right?' when for once you're on top of the world and in the very pink of condition.

Then there is the direct attack. 'You *have* put on weight,' or 'How *thin* you've got' are pronounciamenta which come to other people's lips far too readily, not that the second phrase has ever been, or is indeed likely to be, addressed to me alas!

Another conversational hazard is the identity gambit.

'You're exactly like somebody I used to know in the Army' is a line which tends to make me dislike the speaker at sight, or rather sound. He usually delivers it with a slightly condescending smile and intonation as if he were conferring a great honour on one. He rarely elaborates on the likeness or submits an Identi-kit of his friend's character, but I don't think there is anyone in the world who wants to be told that he (or she) has a double lurking around. There is something spooky in the idea, and the phrase 'spitting image' has never endeared itself to me. Another hopeless and unanswerable opener is: 'It *is* you, isn't it?' usually spoken by a face one has never seen in one's life and hopes never to see again.

Being an actor one is frequently accosted by total strangers who are convinced that they know you personally, having met you on midget screens in lounges, bedrooms or mother-in-law's houses. Usually the encounter starts with a penetrating stare which induces one to think that one may not have adjusted one's dress properly, as is de rigueur in some of the better-class Conveniences. After this the braver specimens advance for a verbal attack.

'I know you, don't I?' is a familiar approach. I tend to remain impassive and totally unhelpful, favouring them nonetheless with a quizzical but wry smile.

After several floundering sentences they usually give up and say, 'I know the face but ...' and their voices trail off, leaving them temporarily at a loss. If they look nice or, I'm afraid, beautiful, I come to their rescue and volunteer my name, but frequently this step is a disaster for both parties. They look even more puzzled and are, I think, convinced that I've given them an alias, and I might tell you that the whole incident isn't inclined to give my morale much of a boost. So I just look sadly at them and slink away, hoping that they may imagine that I'm one of those lovely wrestlers who bite each other on Saturday afternoons, while I am awaiting to check my football pools. Funnily enough I did tell one enquirer that I was Tom Jones and he didn't seem in the least surprised. So anything is possible.

Sometimes the assailant is certain that he (or she) knows more about you and your career than you do yourself and it's a tidge depressing to be assured over and over again that one has been seen in both *Oliver* and *A Man for All Seasons*, when one hasn't in fact even been approached about playing a role in either of these splendid entertainments on stage or screen.

'Oh, but you *were* in it,' the idiots insist, even after I've assured them that they are mistaking me for some other ample character artiste. Quite often it's less exhausting to say, 'All right then. I *was* in it,' which sends *them* happily away anyhow. Or even pretend I'm someone else. I've been Robert Morley, Willoughby Goddard, John Sutro and even Orson Welles more times than I can count.

But in our profession we really are up against it when it comes to the layman (or laywoman if there is such a word) and their idea of what the actor *does*. 'Do you have to do it every night?' (If it happens to be a West End play.) 'Does the make-up hurt?' and 'How do you know when it's your turn to speak?' are typical examples of the questions one is asked at parties and things. Which reminds me of what Dan Massey said to the silly young girl who asked him at a party, 'Don't you get tired of saying the same thing every night?' Replied Mr Massey, 'Yes, don't you?'

And heaven help you if you are in a television programme which has displeased the majority of the viewers. In the days when there were still greengrocers, butchers, florists and fishmongers in my part of the King's Road, Chelsea, I had to be very careful what engagements I accepted, or I'd be greeted by a subsequent storm of abuse.

'The things you do for money nowadays.' 'Fucking awful show you were in last night' and 'Hello Strangler' were comments handed out gratuitously. And sometimes on these occasions one was forced back indoors to face possible starvation. But appear in a popular series and the world was your oyster and at the fishmonger's the reverse was possible.

As a matter of fact there has recently been an upward trend in my relationship with *my* public. Owing to a series of fortuitous circumstances, I was engaged to participate in a commercial for the box to advertise a product called 'Fish Fingers'. The short film was an immediate success and to my huge financial (and of course artistic) delight was shown many times a day. The result was that, although no-one had the faintest idea of my real name, I was immediately identifiable and my stage name was written on many hearts. Daily

I was pursued down the street by urchins yelling, 'There goes good old Commodore Bird's Eye.'

I only hope my most unfavourite non-fan saw it. I ran into him the other month when I was coming out of the laundry, minding my own washing and doing nobody any harm.

''Ello,' said a voice just behind me. I turned to face a cheerful man waiting near the bus stop.

'You 'aven't been very busy lately, 'ave you?' the voice continued.

Now this is the sort of thing which makes me absolutely livid. There is a certain type of viewer who cannot believe there *is* any other medium of entertainment besides the Idiot Box. I explained to the man that an actor did have media outside the small screen in which he could find employment if he was lucky. I hurriedly assured him that I was one of these and during the last year had indeed been exceptionally busy. I'd been starring opposite the Burtons in Hollywood, and had but recently returned from playing the lead in a big Broadway musical. I had a best selling novel just published in the States and was about to condense the life of George Best into a twenty-four part serial.

I stopped this tissue of lies, shaking with rage and clutching my laundry with abandon. There was a pause while he studied me pityingly.

'Yeah,' he said, 'but you 'aven't been on telly, 'ave you?' I felt I should have been in the dock with the Brothers Kray, so guilty did he make me feel. If I'd known what bus he'd been catching I would have pushed him under it and probably ended up in the dock myself. I could see that he was not the man to be impressed by the fact that I was the voice of 'Kattomeat'. I'm frightfully impressed myself.

This disagreeable incident would probably not have happened a few months later when I'd established myself as Commodore Bird's Eye, though I expect he would have mixed me up with Keith Michell in the *Wives of Henry VIII* ... After all they were both costume jobs. Mark you

I like the idea of being easily identifiable as Commodore Bird's Eye and I only hope the Fish Fingers people do too and will whirl me off again one day to the Barbados to shoot Episode Two. After all I'm well known for my interpretations of service gentlemen. For a long time I was Colonel Ironmonger. Oh, didn't you know? Well it all started like this:

There was, and indeed still is, an excellent entertainment guide called *What's On In London*. It has been in existence for many years and has a gossip column giving news of future productions both on stage and screen. It also mentions actors and actresses fairly frequently and at one point certain names seemed to appear regularly and I got a tiny bit exasperated by this, possibly because mine never featured. An actor who seemed to get more than his share of publicity was Martin Benson. He always appeared to have not only one job in the offing but several. Phrases which started off, 'Martin Benson cannot make up his mind whether to ... or ...' were not likely to cause the out of work actor to rub his hands in glee. So I decided to have a bit of fun, though I have nothing against Mr Benson himself, who has written books on acting so he must know what it's all about. I thought I couldn't very easily write to *What's On* under my own name or they'd smell a rat, so one fine day I decided to become Colonel Ironmonger.

It was the Colonel who wrote to the magazine to say that he had but recently returned to England after a long period of service in the Far East and could *What's On* possibly help him? He and his wife were avid theatregoers and would very much like to find out where a particular favourite of theirs, Martin Benson, was appearing. They had, of course, followed his film career with interest in various camp cinemas and had speculated as to whether he was or was not related to the late Sir Frank Benson, the distinguished cricketer-actor-manager. Had *What's On* an answer to his enquiries?

Yes, it had, and a letter came whizzing back saying exactly what Mr Benson was doing at that very moment and in the months to come. This early success went to both the Colonel's and my head and after that there was no holding us. I felt a wonderful sense of power in having an alter ego entirely at my disposal. I suppose that Baron Frankenstein must have undergone a similar emotion when he created another being out of nothing.

But haven't some of *you* wanted to record on paper your indignation at a person or persons, and been stopped from doing so by a desire to remain anonymous? There you are, with your poison-pen poised in mid-air and suddenly you realize that you'd rather not put *your* name at the bottom of the page. And yet it seems rather abortive and weak to sign it 'Disgusted', 'Mother of Eight', 'Livid' or 'Ill Wisher'. In any case the chances of getting a reply to such a missive are remote, and you would have to face some pretty peculiar looks from the postman when he delivered a bundle of mail to 'Mr Livid', 'I. Wisher Esq.', etc.

So I'd advise you to do what I did. I gave birth, quite painlessly, to a retired Colonel, and for a time we were inseparable. We shared the same joys, sorrows and indeed, club. In order not to arouse suspicion, I deemed it wiser for him to have a residence of his own, and I decided to make him a member of a club. From its safe precincts he could deal with his correspondence and collect the replies. For weeks on end he could be seen scribbling away in the writing room and it was sometimes an embarrassment when I called in at the Club Post Office to ask for my mail.

'No, Commander Bull,' the custodian was apt to reply, 'but there's quite a bit of stuff for your friend Colonel Ironmonger.'

Although most of his early letters contained complaints or adverse comments on policy, our targets increased their range and some of the despatches were of a genial and unprovocative nature. The Colonel started on an interesting investigation into the prevalence of a new type of chiff-chaff that year in Chalfont St Giles, and the astonishing size of vegetable marrows suddenly appearing at Mitcham, which caused a plethora of excited interest among gardening enthusiasts.

Every now and then though the Colonel felt impelled to give a sharp rap over the knuckles to someone or other who had provoked him unfavourably by word, thought or deed. If a genuine grievance needed airing he was the first to gird up his loins and strike, whether it was to ameliorate the catering arrangements at some of the London suburban stations, or draw attention to certain irregularities in the conduct of the Wigan branch of the Society for the Prevention of Over-polishing of Dumb Waiters.

One of his favourite hobby horses was dealing with errors of print. A weekly magazine, devoted entirely to the pursuit of pleasure, recklessly announced an Alec Guinness season at one of the Classic Repertory Cinemas. Among the films to be shown were *The Lavender Hill Mob*, 7 March for four days, *The Man in the White Suit*, 11 March for three days, and *Oliver Twist* 14 March for four *years*.

The Colonel felt that he could not let this astonishingly improbable announcement go unchallenged. With a brisk rattle of spurs, he took up his ball-pointed lance and rushed into the lists to face the Editor of the magazine.

Sir,

There seems to be some confusion about the programme of the Classic Cinema, as announced in last week's issue. I rang up the place of entertainment in question to reserve two seats for the film *Oliver Twist* for 23 March 1964. The good lady in the box-office told me she couldn't be certain that this particular film would be showing on this date. Yet I read in your excellent journal that *Oliver Twist* would be at the Classic Cinema for four years, commencing 14 March 1960.

It is really extremely aggravating as I wanted the evening to be a surprise for Mrs Ironmonger, as, by a curious coincidence, the outing would take place exactly ten years after the day on which we got engaged, while we were witnessing this identical film. This auspicious occasion took place at the Camp Theatre in Darjeeling, where I happened to be stationed at the time.

So you can understand that, for sentimental reasons, it is essential to ascertain whether you or the lady supposedly in charge of the arrangements at the Classic Cinema have Right on your side.

Yours etc.,

F. Ironmonger, Lieut-Col. (retired)

Unfortunately the offending magazine paid little attention to this cri de coeur and replied shortly but blandly that there had been a printing error. Apparently 'four years' should have read 'four days'. The journal did, however, take the opportunity of wishing the Colonel and his lady every happiness.

The Colonel, nothing daunted, returned to his Club writing room and got cracking about the nutritive properties of carrot juice. He had visited a tribe in the Eastern Himalayas who subsisted entirely on the stuff.

I myself was appearing around this time in a so-called entertainment called *Waiting for Godot* and we were having a bit of trouble one way and another. It was a play which was having a dreadful effect on the actors and I found myself becoming paranoic and afflicted with persecution mania. I managed to persuade Colonel Ironmonger, who loathed the play, to write letters to Mr Donald Albery, our manager, Mr Peter Hall, our director, and the *Evening Standard*. I think it was all about an Awards dinner, or lunch and, though the play won something set up by the newspaper, none of the cast had been invited to the festivities. So the Colonel got frightfully cross about it and once more entered the lists. None of the addressees replied though Peter Hall did confess to me some time later that he'd put the letter in his 'Too difficult to answer' file.

This sort of thing kept the Colonel pretty busy and he did become very much part of the London scene and even struck up a delightful pen-palship with Mr Harold Hobson, that doyen of dramatic critics. This is how it came about. Mr H. H., as all the theatrical world knows, is not entirely impervious to the charms and talent of Mme Edwidge Feuillère. It so happens that I played a tiny part in a film starring the illustrious French actress and Mr Stewart Granger. It was called *Woman Hater* and I referred to it briefly in an earlier tome. One day, to my astonishment, I got a note from Mr Hobson asking if I'd lunch with him and discuss the work of Mme Feuillère in the film, as he was writing a book about her career. I wrote back instanter, pointing out that I would be breaking bread with him under false pretences. The only contact I had had with the actress was when I'd said '*Bon Jour, Madame*' to her on the set. To which she'd replied '*Bon Jour* to you'. I had then disappeared to rehearse a scene with Miss Irene Handl about whose work I was prepared to talk at length as I've admired it so tremendously through the years.

Mr Hobson replied that it was a strange coincidence but he *happened* to be writing a book about Miss Handl the moment he'd finished the one he was writing about the French lady and would I have lunch with him at the Caprice the following Thursday, so I said I would.

Those were the days when quite a lot of actors and actresses (working) could afford to go to this restaurant, and I found, on following Mr Hobson in, that several friends of mine were staring at us in amazement.

'I'll explain on the blower,' I hissed at them as I passed. You see, all actors rather think of critics as 'Them' on the other side of the footlights and rarely get mixed up with them socially. But they do have very definite views about their writing.

'He doesn't know anything about the theatre,' they say, until 'he' happens to write something nice about 'them' or the play they are in.

'I think he's really rather good these days,' the fickle artiste is liable to announce.

Anyhow I had a very jolly lunch with Mr Hobson, who had been not 'rather' but 'frightfully' good about my theatre books.

'He really is frightfully good,' I kept saying, particularly as he doesn't mind my sending up *Waiting for Godot* which is his theatrical bible. What is so endearing about him is that he is a real enthusiast for the theatre and he will always find *something* worth while in an evening which for other critics appears to have no redeeming feature. I found myself being wildly indiscreet about both managements and artistes. Finally, for some unknown reason, I told him about Colonel Ironmonger. This apparently tickled him and for some weeks afterwards both my Alter Ego's and my life were enlivened by Mr Hobson's letters to him.

Unfortunately the whole thing was becoming all too public and as a result F. F. Ironmonger (Lieut-Col. retired) was losing his usefulness. I finally had to announce his sudden demise. The funeral service was quite simple and was held at the RAC. The ashes were distributed into one of the waste-paper baskets which, as some cynics point out, the late Colonel used all too infrequently. I found it curious that there was no reference to his passing in the newspapers to which he had so assiduously contributed during his lifetime.

After his death I found among his papers a letter addressed to him from a well-known film magazine. I opened it eagerly. It was a reply to a question which the Colonel had put to their reference columns. He had asked quite simply, 'What *has* happened to Peter Bull?' Unfortunately they told him and the news may have hastened his death.

But his spirit lives on and those of you who have noticed letters in the press or even been on the receiving end of communications from Admiral Sir Douglas Forsyth (Rear, of course) may detect a familiar ring about the attitudes struck. The fact that he is a member of the same club may also give a clue.

Although, as you are sick of hearing, I'm not all that

keen on the actual acting, I do like pretending to be somebody else, and to assume someone else's personality in what is called 'real life' attracts me enormously.

That is why it amazes me how cross people get when I have dialled the wrong number in error, or sometimes, I have to admit, as a result of sheer carelessness. From the tone of their voice you would think either (a) that I had done it on purpose, (b) that I was a spy employed by the UnBritish Activities Tribunal or (c) that I was about to say something obscene. The last supposition is the only reasonable one as far as I am concerned, as, not only do I read about that sort of thing in the dear old-fashioned *News of the World*, but I have been on the receiving end myself. But more of that anon, if not anonymously.

But, you see, I feel totally different if I pick up the receiver and find that someone has dialled *me* by mistake. A fierce sense of exhilaration steals over me and I am instantly transplanted like Walter Mitty into a fantastic and fascinating world. I find myself changing in front of my very own eyes into the person or persons required.

'Is that the Sub-Standard Laundry?' they ask.

'Oh yes, indeed,' I find myself replying with glee, 'and what can I do for you, Sir or Madam?' And immediately I find myself involved in some trauma about missing sheets or torn combinations. I settle their fears by telling them that, though there has been a small fire, their things are perfectly safe. To vary it, sometimes I say that leprosy has broken out among the staff, but it's well under control now, and then the client can relax for the day.

Not only do I spread calm but I also encourage trade.

'Offal is particularly good,' I say to the housewife who has mistaken me for her butcher, 'but I would advise you to pay us an early visit as there is bound to be a run on it.'

I suppose the real reason for my enjoying this kind of lunatic behaviour is that I am a casual labourer and therefore have unlimited time at my disposal. And if by error I do happen to have something important to do, it's lovely to be able to leave it and have a good frivol. (Perfectly good word. The Fowler brothers are mad about it.) As a result the telephone has only to ring once for me to bound across the room to cope with any emergency.

'Is that Reg?'

'Yes,' I say hopefully.

'It doesn't sound like Reg.'

'Well, I've got a bit of a cold,' I parry. But usually they are off the wire before I have found out if they wanted Reg to marry them, give them a thousand pounds, murder their mother or take them to *The Mousetrap*.

Sometimes the caller gets quite cross. I was sitting quiet as a mouse at home one day when the phone went.

'Hello,' I said.

'Hello,' said The Other. 'Is it a black tie or white one?' I thought for a minute.

'I don't really know,' I replied.

'Well it says on the invitation card.'

'Isn't it on yours?' I asked, thinking how clever I was being.

'I've lost mine you idiot,' said the voice, 'that's why I'm ringing you. Go and have a look at yours.'

'O.K.,' I mumbled. I realized that this might be a genuine conversation stopper. I returned after about three minutes.

'I say, I'm most frightfully sorry,' I said in my best Deb dance voice, 'but I seem to have lost mine too.'

Other End was apoplectic with rage.

'Christ,' it said, 'you might have been quicker.' Then, 'I say, that is Alec isn't it?'

'No,' I said with what I fear amounted to a simper. 'It's Peter as a matter of fact!'

He rang off and a few seconds later the phone went again. I decided to take a chance.

'How do you know we *have* to dress?' I asked. 'It might be a nudist party or Drag.'

I heard a groan from the other end.

'Oh, it's not fucking you again is it?' and he slammed the receiver down.

But every now and again I find someone willing to play the game my way and an extended and unforeseen conversation with a stranger is not only possible, but can transport one to mysterious realms of fantasy and delight.

For instance I have the good fortune to have a telephone number similar to that of the Classic Cinema Chelsea, so I get involved in some highly risible situations. The other day a lady phoned.

'Can you tell me what you've got on today?' she asked.

'Grey flannels and a rather nice lambswool coat I got off the peg at Harrods' sale,' I replied.

There was a gurgling laugh from the other end of the blower.

'You are *awful,*' the lady said, 'you aren't the Chelsea Classic at all.'

'Well, I'm not actually the Chelsea Classic, but don't hang up because I do happen to know what's on there.'

Silence from the other end and I pursued my advantage.

'It's an early Bardot and the stills outside look jolly sexy, I don't mind telling you.'

'Do they?' she commented severely, and I can't tell you how enchanting she sounded, 'Doubtless you know then what time the film comes on.'

'But of course,' I said. '2, 4, 6, 8, 10. The news is at 1.50, 3.50, 5.50, 7.50, and 9.50. I'll meet you outside at 1.45, 3.45, 5.45, 7.45 or 9.45.'

There was a pause in our conversation. Then,

'The ghastly thing is that I've promised to go with my husband this evening.'

'Make him take you somewhere else,' I said, '*Carry on Scuba Diving* is on at the Odeon.'

'No. I can't. He *loves* the Classic and hates to go anywhere else. But you do sound rather nice.'

'Actually I'm a sex maniac,' I announced, 'but don't let that put you off.'

'It doesn't,' she reassured me, 'but I can't sit here all day waffling to you, pleasant as it's been. Good-bye.'

'No, no. Don't go yet,' I cried at her. 'You must get hold of the right number of the Classic. Got a pencil and paper?'

She had, and there and then I gave her *my* number but she hasn't rung since.

Other diversions to be practised with the help of Mr Alexander Bell's delightful wheeze include finding oneself the third party in a conversation which has been going on happily and undisturbed for some time. One has lifted one's own phone for a perfectly legitimate call and finds that a parley is already in full spate. Here, to get the full benefit of this stroke of luck, it is advisable to bide one's time until a suitable moment and then throw in a well-placed comment. This surprises the original participants.

'Did you say something?' they ask one another.

'No I thought it was you.'

'There must be something wrong with the phone.'

'I think he's gone now,' says the more hopeful one. And I remain speechless for a suitable period and then let fly.

Requests ranging from 'Do you mind hanging up? You are on our line,' to the most frightful expletives, come cracking down the phone. Of course I *mind* hanging up. Sometimes I do a very quick click to make them *think* I am no longer there but in fact I remain glued to the receiver and soak in the usually useless bits of information being dished out. A real Listening Tom, that's me. Right at the end I pop in a 'Good-bye. I have so much enjoyed our little chat. Hear from you both again soon, I hope,' which, I would think, unsettles them for the rest of the day. Silly fools. If only they had some guts they would ring off and try another line. I might not be able to lurk on that one.

Sometimes the speakers are so irritating that I can hardly restrain myself. I picked up the phone once and heard a young gent talking to a very South Kensington type of young lady. The conversation was desultory in the extreme. The man was making all the running and the girl was obviously frightfully bored but had nothing else to do. Neither could be classed as a brilliant conversationalist.

'So how did you get home last night?'

'You remember that old Colonel with the gammy leg who would do the Twist?'

'Yes.'

'He drove me home.'

'He didn't!'

'Yes, he did.'

'But he was pissed.'

'Yes, he was a bit. But I couldn't get out of it. He's an old friend of Mummy's. It's my Worst Thing.'

'What is?'

'People being pissed.'

'Yes. It's my Worst Thing, too.'

There was a longish pause. Then the girl thought she must say something.

'How did *you* get home?'

'You remember that big woman in blue. I had to drive her back to Richmond.'

'What was her name?'

'I never found out but I think she arranges flowers for the Queen Mother.'

I thought that was my cue.

'Goodness gracious,' I said, 'that's quite a conversation stopper.' And indeed it was. There was an interim before the girl said, 'Did you say something about a conversation stopper?'

'No, I didn't,' he said.

'I did,' I said.

She said, 'There's someone on the line, I think.' I bided my time and kept quiet while they went on discussing the Mysterious Voice. Then,

'I think they've gone.'

'Yes. So do I.'

'What were you saying before we were interrupted?'

'I can't remember.'

I thought it was time to assist.

'You were talking about the lady who arranged the flowers for the Queen Mother,' I prompted.

'Oh it's too bad,' said the girl. 'He's on the line again.'

'Let's ignore him,' said her friend. And so they did. They went chuntering on in an aimless fashion until the girl, when asked by the man what she was going to do that week-end answered,

'I'm going down to Daddy.'

'You're not!' I interposed, deeply shocked. 'How disgusting!' This threw them into a bit of a turmoil and I decided to remain mousey quiet until I looked at my watch some ten minutes later.

'Look here,' I broke in on them, 'you've made me late for dinner. It was quite the most boring conversation I've ever heard in my life and I do wish you wouldn't be so thoughtless.' I burst into floods of tears and then put my phone down quietly.

I am bound to admit that I have had my share of anonymous phone calls but only in one case did they have continuity and during my association I found myself turning into a lady called Phyllis.

It all started as a result of a conversation with my 'daily' whom I found purse-lipped when I returned from a shopping spree.

'Mr Bull, I think you ought to get on to Scotland Yard at once,' she announced.

'Why, Mrs Pye?' I asked. 'Have we been burgled?'

'No, sir, but there's been this terrible man on the phone saying horrible things.'

'What sort of things?' I asked, thrilled to the marrow.

'Oh sir, I couldn't bring myself to tell *you*, sir, but it was all about knickers and measurements,' she said darkly.

'Leave it to me, Mrs Pye,' I said, trying desperately to recall whether one had to dial 100 instead of 999, as one seems to have to do now for everything.

But, what with lunch and the washing-up I forgot all

about it until later in the day, when the phone rang several times in fairly quick succession. I kept on picking up the bloody thing and saying 'Hello' cordially, but all the reply I got was some rather asthmatic breathing, and the click of a replaced instrument. It was not a highly satisfactory form of intercourse, and was nothing to do with the Generation Gap. I realized that I was dealing with what is described in the courts as a Breacher of the Peace.

It must be pointed out before we go further or indeed too far, that I was at this time living in a flat recently vacated by a charming actress, whose name had remained in the telephone directory long after she'd left the building. Her engagement had just been announced in *The Times* and other newspapers, and these two combined facts were responsible for the confusion which was to engulf me for the next few weeks or so.

Anyhow, the next time the phone rang I decided to teach the caller a tiny lesson. I answered him in a ladylike way. This caused my unknown communicator to open his trap for the first time. He asked me if I was Phyllis. I admitted that it was indeed my name. He then went straight into the attack. Did my fiancé know I was not a virgin and that he (the caller) had had me innumerable times. I simulated outrage in a high falsetto, which is frightfully tiring, and then he proceeded to make about ten not frightfully old-fashioned suggestions about what he'd like to do to me, or rather dear old Phyllis.

It would be hypocritical to pretend that I was remotely shocked. I found it, I have to admit, rather erotic and jokey to a degree. I let him prattle on happily, every now and then throwing in an 'Oh but you mustn't say things like that!' or 'Stop it!' 'You're disgusting.' Anyhow, he finally rang off, obviously deeply satisfied, and that was that.

Well it wasn't as a matter of fact. He was on the blower frequently and was so persistent that I thought out a plan to Teach Him A Lesson. Such was his ardour that I was convinced that I might be able to entice him round to see me in person. Little fool that I was! I didn't realize then that the only thrill these kind of people (sneer! sneer!) get out of it is the fact that they can't be seen and can *imagine* their effect on the person they are persecuting. In those days I was nowhere near as sophisticated in these matters as I am now, so I thought that it was up to me to keep him on a string, or in this case a bit of tangled cord. At the right moment I would issue an invitation and then, when he rang my bell (front door), I'd be there and usher him in, saying graciously,

'I'm Phyllis. Do come in. It's so nice to *see* you and not hear you for a change.'

After carefully closing the door to prevent his flight I'd introduce him to the small but select audience whom I would have assembled there.

But he proved difficult to pin down and for over two weeks my life was turned upside down. What with answering everyone, including my aged mother and my agent (no, they're not the same person, you fool!) in a falsetto voice, there was complete disruption in the home, not helped by my more tasteless friends ringing up pretending to be what Mr Tennessee Williams might describe as my Gentleman Caller.

Some of the ordinary people who phoned me during this period hurriedly put the phone down, thinking I'd either had a disastrous accident or gone potty, and any prospective employers were frightened away. Things couldn't go on like this as none of our nerves would stand it. I decided it had gone far enough.

At a particularly unsuitable moment during the night, the blower went and My Caller asked me if I'd had my bath and was I wearing anything under my housecoat. For some reason he was mad about housecoats. I replied in a falsetto that I wasn't even wearing a housecoat, which sent him, I imagine, into a frenzy of excitement.

'Oh,' he said, 'haven't you had your bath yet?'

'As a matter of fact,' I replied, 'I haven't. In any case I'm going to shave first.'

There was a gasp from the other end of the blower.

'So sucks to you,' I said, speaking in my normal voice.

'And double sucks,' I added in a falsetto.

I heard a groan and that was the end of this not frightfully savoury episode. All rather sad, really.

5. *Perilous Journey*

DURING the latter years of her long life, my mother used to pop off to a nice country-house hotel near Heathfield in Sussex. She dreaded her 'holiday', and it was only at the pistol point of domestic necessity that she could bring herself to leave her comfortable Chelsea flat. Yet once she had arrived in her place of exile she settled down fairly happily, as her hosts were kind and genuinely fond of her. In fact everything went swimmingly during the entire three weeks, as long as no-one required a bath at the same time as my mother. Her interest in new residents was not confined to their appearance or even their love life, but almost exclusively to what time they *looked* like wanting to have a bath.

Preparations for her departure were elaborate and intensive and started many weeks before. Everything was planned on a military scale and it was no fault of hers or her faithful maid Jessie that what should have been quite a simple operation was marred every time by unforeseen perils.

Her Exodus in her eighty-seventh year was a typical example. For several years previously she had caught, with about an hour to spare, the 10.38 to Heathfield from Victoria, but never without some hair-raising hazard. The year before she was put by a nonchalant porter in the wrong half of the train and had had to change at Eridge, wherever that might be. One year she was deliberately dispatched protesting on the 10.8. It got to Heathfield very much earlier, but it threw my mother, who had contracted with herself to catch the 10.38.

I used to pick her up in a taxi at 09.45 hours.

('That should give us plenty of time, dear.') And indeed it did. It enabled us to arrive at Victoria Station well before 10.00 hours, when there was scant chance of the train condescending to show its dear little face on the platform.

The trek on this occasion had started off well enough with the trapping of an amiable but bemused taxi-gent, who had just finished transporting an eccentric lady client. She had apparently asked him what she owed.

'Three shillings and sixpence, Madam,' he said civilly enough, but the lady had flown into a rage, and shouted, 'You are insulting! How do you know that I am married?' The driver had wisely held his peace but was obviously relieved to pick up a fairly normal consignment like the mater and me.

We arrived at the Buckingham Palace entrance to the station in the highest of spirits at 09.52 hours, and if I hadn't had my mother's horoscope for the day engraven on my brain, I would have imagined that all boded well. It had read, 'A puzzling day. Special compensations await after tea.'

There were two porters ready to take the luggage, whom I shall have to christen Porter A and Porter B. They have leading parts in the ensuing drama and do not deserve to linger in the memory anonymously.

'What train, Madam?' asked Porter A cordially.

'The 10.38 to Heathfield,' replied my mother.

Porter A looked at Porter B with consternation written all over his face.

'There is no such train, Madam,' he said.

'Nonsense,' replied my mother. 'I booked my seat on it at the Army and Navy stores yesterday.'

Both porters were visibly rattled by this piece of intelligence but Porter B replied.

'There is a 10.8 and a 11.8 to Heathfield,' he said helpfully but ungrammatically.

'But the Army and Navy,' reiterated my mother, 'told me that the 10.38 was definitely running.'

'You should have checked with *our* enquiries, Madam,' chimed in Porter A re-entering the fray.

A short silence followed, only to be broken by the kindlier Porter B.

'Why not take the 10.8?' he pleaded.

My mother still on her guard but pretty off her porter(s), asked coldly if it went straight through to Heathfield.

'No Madam,' came the reply, 'you would have to change at Eridge.'

'In that case,' said my mother with ill-concealed triumph in her voice, 'I would rather take the 11.8. The Army and Navy told me that *did* go through.'

The porters, to my surprise, did not question this statement and I seized the lull in hostilities to suggest that the luggage should be parked in the cloakroom and that we should have a strong coffee. I did not, however, include Porters A and B in the invitation.

Porter A disappeared with the luggage after a dainty shrug and left us with mixed emotions. Suddenly my mother and I were galvanized by a quiet voice behind us saying:

'Which platform for the 10.38 to Heathfield, please Porter?'

I whipped round to see Porter B staring thunderstruck at a lady in Sensible Tweeds. It was some time before he could pull himself together and then he bawled at his friend Porter A, now deep in conversation with Cloakroom.

'Hold it Bill! Here's another for that 10.38.'

The tone of his voice suggested that Sensible Tweeds and my mother had asked to be transported on a rocket train to the moon and were querying which end the rocket restaurant car would be situated in. Nevertheless Porter A returned to us and dumped my mother's luggage gloomily round and about my feet. He then instructed Porter B to go and enquire. In his absence my mother struck up an immediate and warm friendship with Sensible Tweeds. Discretion was apparently being thrown to the winds and phrases like: 'What *are* things coming to?' and 'What *will* the foreigners think?' came wafting across the station air with crystal clarity.

After what seemed an age we spotted Porter B winging his way wearily over to us, holding a scruffy piece of paper.

'Platform 14,' he announced simply and unaffectedly.

My mother made no comment on this volte face, to my amazement, beyond pointing out that Last Year it had been on Platform 16. A small excited cavalcade (we had now been joined by a lady with a small trim beard, both of whom were bound for Uckfield) shuffled off to Platform 14 where, needless to say, there was no sign of a train and the barriers were tight closed.

The porters dropped the luggage, intending presumably to have a short conference on the mutability of human affairs. Unfortunately they found themselves caught up in the web of uncertainty which seemed to be sweeping Victoria Station like a forest fire. Passengers from nowhere descended on them for information, little knowing that they could not have picked two more unreliable authorities.

At long last a gentleman appeared from a trap-door inside the platform and opened the barriers. As we surged forwards he hurriedly closed them. But to compensate for the disappointment he did insert a destination board into the socket provided. It read 'Front part Uckfield. Rear part Heathfield'.

I turned to my mother with relief. 'Well dear, that looks all right,' I said.

'Last year,' she replied coldly, 'it was the other way round and I got into the wrong part and had to change at Eridge.'

Before I had time to work this out, the barriers opened and we were allowed on to the platform just in time to receive the onslaught of several hundred tardy daily-breaders who were disgorged by an angry-looking train. They knocked a suitcase and one porter sideways, but luckily not the mater who stood her ground. She surveyed the train with disfavour.

'What a dirty train,' she commented.

'It's probably not the right one,' I said facetiously and a second later I could have bitten off my tiny tongue. For looking back at the barrier I saw a hand stretch out and withdraw the destination board on which all our hopes were centred.

'I don't want to seem too inquisitive,' I said to Porter B, 'but why have they taken down that board?' I had by now established a sort of relationship with both porters owing to the fact that they had seen me recently as the villain in a wildly unsuitable film called *Dead Men's Shoes*.

Porter B loped off to the barrier and spoke to an Unknown Spokesman for British Railways. He returned with his cheeks suffused by a blush which certainly suited the sensational announcement that he was about to make.

'Platform 15,' he said in a fine clear voice.

My mother, to my astonishment, started to giggle and I loved her very dearly at that moment. Her only comment, before sounding the retreat, was to repeat her assertion that last year it had been platform 16.

Platform 15 was, of course, quite empty when we arrived and we hovered just inside the barrier awaiting fresh instructions. A very large lady in what appeared to be a Russian uniform, suddenly appeared from outer space.

'Anyonepunchedyourtickets?' she asked.

'Pardon,' I asked.

'Anyonepunchedyourtickets?' she repeated.

'Oh yes,' I replied airily, 'dozens of people. By the way does the 10.38 for Heathfield go from this platform?'

'Dunnoitisn'tinyet,' she said, which on reflection did not seem to be a statement which was going to help anybody very much.

We stood there irresolutely and then a train came quietly into the platform and a lot of passengers got out. No-one got knocked over at all and there was a certain calmness all round.

'It's a steam one,' said my mother for no apparent reason. Three passengers, two porters and I mounted the train, whose carriages were strewn with newspapers. The three passengers were Sensible Tweeds, Trim Beard and my mother. It was becoming increasingly obvious that the 10.38 had no appeal for passing trade and, let's face it, no wonder.

I gave Porter A a good deal of money and he went away. I sat down beside my mother and she suddenly looked very small and frail and I wanted to go all the way with her, in case of fresh confusion. I wished also that I could stop thinking about a play called *The Ghost Train.*

'I'm sorry to fuss so,' said my mother out of the blue, 'but could you just have a word with the engine driver?'

I girded up my bedraggled loins and walked down the platform to the Engine, which was serving dainty cups of tea to its inhabitants. I asked it if it was thinking of going to Heathfield.

'No,' it said, but couching the information in a rather more definite form. 'Try the other end.'

I ambled down the far end of the train which seemed to be stationed hard by Clapham Junction, but I could see no sign of a locomotive. I returned to the mater who had settled down fairly cosily to the remains of somebody else's *Daily Telegraph.* I hadn't the heart to tell her of the new anxiety. I think she guessed my predicament because she said,

'You go now dear. I'm sure I'll be all right.'

The words were hardly out of her mouth before the train started off with a jerk and I rushed from it like a streak of rather rusty lightning. I slammed the door and looked back into the carriage for the last time. I caught a glimpse of the bravest old lady I ever knew and I can't swear to it but I think she was giggling again. She waved gaily as she left on the 10.38, bound, I assured myself, for Heathfield.

Later I heard that she'd arrived safely, but I never checked up to see if her horoscope had come true and that she did indeed receive 'special compensations after tea'.

I always meant to write a book about my mother but after doing one about my father, thought it wiser not. In fact I didn't really write that one but culled the whole thing from the diaries he so meticulously kept for himself and his four sons. After I had covered ten years of his life (1912, the year I was born, to 1922) I thought I'd better show the proofs to those most immediately concerned. I asked the mater if she had any complaints.

'Yes dear,' she said, 'I changed from petticoats to knickers in 1913 not 1912 and I'm a rising 87 not 88.' I remarked that by the time the book eventually came out she would be the latter.

'Anything else?' I enquired.

'No, dear,' she replied, 'but you're going to have a bit of trouble with the boys.' 'The boys' turned out to be my two surviving brothers, aged 50 and 52 respectively.

They did complain, quite justifiably in some cases, about my sensational revelations of our childhood life in The Meadows, a large house in the Uxbridge Road, where I spent the first 18 years of my life. Hence the title of the book *Bulls in the Meadows*. But the reaction they had to the book warned me not to attempt anything similar for a bit. So it is with a sense of relief that I can report on the Annual Reunion of the Old Norlanders, which is the name under which the ex-pupils of the Norland Place High School in Holland Park are disguised. All the Bull boys were there at one time or another, but in 1971 I was the only representative of the family present at the reunion.

How refreshing it is to find small pockets of resistance against the swirling waters of progress these days. For instance, take Beatons the Bakers in the King's Road, Chelsea, a locality where nearly every shop has changed hands twice in the last few years. Yet here the same exquisitely mannered ladies are still dispensing delicious bread and home-made cakes, seemingly unperturbed by the hideous cacophony of noise blaring from the neighbouring boutiques.

I love going there (when I'm not on a diet) just to soak in the atmosphere; and it's a Comfort that it hasn't altered through the post-war decades. It was with the same sense of desire for reassurance that I climbed down the narrow-winding staircase leading to the Drill Hall of the Kindergarten School, still flourishing after nearly a hundred years of service. It is half a century since I was a pupil but the Annual Reunion brings back my days there most vividly. To return there now requires a bit of courage on my part as I tend to be the only male present.

The establishment caters mainly for girls, and boys are still only permitted to stay there when they are very young. As a result of this preponderance of females, I found my recent professional activities listed in the School Magazine under the heading of 'News of Old Girls' which raised a few eyebrows. But now that the stigma of a possible sex-change has been lifted, I am made very welcome and, once I am there, enjoy the fiesta hugely.

We are advised some weeks before The Happening by the admirably efficient secretary of the Association who signs all her communications Phyllis Parsons, Flight Officer (Retired). A handsome blonde lady, it is she who dispenses the Raffle Tickets, reads the Minutes and flogs the sandwiches and cakes (if any) left untouched at the end of the festivities. These have been constructed by our Committee and are delicious. They have little flags on them to denote the constituents like 'Cod's Roe', 'Cheese and Chutney' or 'Cake' (Dundee).

Sometimes I think a lot of us only come for the tea which is a substantial affair and this year was enlivened by the Great Teapot Scandal, when the spout got clogged and Miss Hobson, our Chairman, and others had to dole the stuff out in cups dipped into the pot itself. Miss Hobson! Ah! She taught me over fifty years ago and still looks, as Miss Parsons put in her affectionate and witty Report, 'as though she had just come off the hockey field'. In my day there I was terrified of her but sat in adoration trying to win her praise. My father wrote a poem for me to present to her, the ingratiating theme of which was 'I strive to be Miss Hobson's Choice'.

One of the riveting attractions of these reunions is to observe the seeming indestructibility of both Miss Hobson and her colleague, Miss Harvey. Their memory is phenomenal and I can't hope to catch Miss Hobson out, however hard I try. 'Oh no, Peter! You've got it all wrong. Cynthia Fairweather went to Ceylon not Cyprus. In the fifties. Seems quite happy.' I ask her news of other little girls I fancied in 1920, having done my homework with old diaries and school lists. She is able to fill in the time gaps for most of them, though I still can't contact Barbara Sturges, the Apple of my Eye, last heard of Alive and Kicking teaching at Roedean, but who has obstinately refused to contact me, even after the paeon of praise I lifted to her in *Bulls in the Meadows.** However *tant pis*, as I think they say somewhere.

After a long chat with 'The Hobber', as she likes to be called, I find myself being attacked by a mature matron, who affirms that she sat next to me in Geography. 'What are you going to do about *Tom Jones?*' she demands accusingly. It appears that she has taken her grandchildren to a reissue of the film at the local Odeon and the colour print and/or the projection were not up to standard. I try to convince her that it's hardly the business of a supporting actor to ensure the quality of the negative of a ten-year-old movie but she refuses to be mollified.

Fortunately at this moment Miss Hobson rings her little tinkly gold bell and we all sit down in the hall, which, apart from a new War Memorial plaque, has remained unchanged

* As we go to press I am happy to report that at last Miss Sturges has surfaced. A brief but happy reunion was engineered by my niece Charlotte, herself an alumna from Miss S.'s Academy of Teaching near Brighton. This happy event took place not a very large stone's throw from Norland Place. *Tant mieux!*

from the days when I did gym, sang hymns, listened to Speech Days and made instant friends and enemies there. Even the slightly musty smell is evocative.

Proceedings open with the singing of the school hymn 'He who would Valiant Be'. The one masculine voice blends in a most sinister way and I soon desist, being unable to carry out the premise of the title. Later, a motion is put to the members to substitute a new composition, which a member of the Committee kindly plays for us on the pianoforte, which looks suspiciously like the one I remember from 1921. Written by the current Singing and Music Mistress at the Norland Place High School and Kindergarten, it contains the stanza:

'For Health and Strength and Happy Hours enjoyed at Norland Place,
We thank thee, Lord, for Blessing Us and Giving of Thy Grace.'

It didn't of course, stand a chance with us Old Philistines and nor did Miss Hobson's offer to resign as Chairman. Apparently there is a bye-law in the constitution of the Association which forbids the continuation of chairmanship after a certain period. Miss Hobson has nevertheless been at the helm as long as I can remember.

There were yells of 'No! No!' Pandemonium broke loose and finally she had to ring her Chairman's bell to restore order. It was obvious that not a single Old Girl or *the* single Old Boy wanted anything changed for the next fifty years. After this had been made perfectly clear, we settled down to the serious business of the day which included the report on the Wine and Cheese Bring and Buy party in the summer, how much had accrued in our Post Office Savings Account and news of a handsome bequest from an Old Girl.

Everybody thanked everyone, the winners of the Raffle collected their prizes, the surplus sandwiches went like hot cakes, some of us became a bit misty-eyed as we bade farewell to Madam Chairman and each other, but we all filed out in an orderly fashion to Holland Park, feeling warmed by the nostalgic atmosphere of the afternoon's events. Though I couldn't help wishing that my beloved Nanny had been there to meet me and take my hand.

Nanny, with whom I was in love for many years, natch, was a Miss Ethel Williams, whose departure from The Meadows left our whole family bereft and caused my father to write an ode on the tragedy. But she had a desire 'to travel' and became a member of the Nannies' Jet Set, until settling down into marriage with Teddy Denn, a distinguished officer in the Merchant Navy.

She never lost interest in all of us Bull boys and followed my theatrical career with its ups and downs intently. And, goodness me, there were some downs.

6. *For Puck's Sake*

BEFORE graduating to some rather classy films, I managed by hook, and indeed with crooks, to get into a great many very bad ones. A highlight, I suppose, was one in which I played a character called Clarkson, a ghastly well-fed villain who wore red carnations and kept on hitting his mistress, played with élan by Miss Sheilagh Fraser. Entitled *Salute the Toff* it was quite a collector's item. It was shot simultaneously with another of the series called *Hammer the Toff* which used the same furniture, a certain proportion of the same dialogue, and sometimes the same artistes, though not unfortunately in my case. I never saw the finished product but eye-witnesses reported on its risibility risk from audiences.

After my upgrading, in spite of the increase in my bank balance and as a result in my morale, I did, at the back of my subconscious, rather miss the dottiness, desperation and hysteria of the good old 'quickie' days.

A year or so ago I informed my agents that I was prepared to do *anything* (professionally that is) for money, as I had a month to fill in before leaving for my annual sojourn in Greece. As I'd turned down one or two big movies which would have interfered with the summer schedule they were fairly bewildered.

However, it landed me one spring morning in a fairly sinister flat off the Edgware Road, where the offices of Puck Films seemed to be located at the time. The company was about to embark on a production called *Licensed To Kill* which was intended to be a satire on the James Bond series. It didn't seem the moment to point out that all films *were* those days, and I hastily accepted the role of Masterman, a master mind, who was to provide me with a two-day guarantee and a hundred pounds in the kitty. My agents intimated that they thought I was out of my mind (not for the first time).

The director-cum-author was a sensitive and highly nervous young Canadian called Lindsay Shonteff, who resembled a greyhound just before being released from its trap. Little did he know how many hurdles and water-jumps were lurking round the corner.

The person who seemed to hold the financial and production reins was an intimidating lady called Estelle Richmond, a name which would have suited a fragile silent film star down to the ground. Silent Miss Richmond wasn't and, when she wasn't on the blower haggling over the last penny, she was dealing with a series of Incidents which dogged the making of *Licensed To Kill*. Anyhow, she gave me a script and I hied myself to the Royal Automobile Club to 'study' same. Although it's a common phrase among actors 'I'm going home to study', I've rarely been conscious of doing it myself. I usually read it, stare at it, throw it in the corner, stare at it, curse it, learn it and forget it. But for some unknown reason I did 'study' my part in *Licensed To Kill* and jolly glad I was that I did. I had been told that they hoped to shoot the whole of the Masterman scenes in the Hilton Hotel and some graveyard or other. I suppose it was the interesting combination of locations that led me into the abyss. Because, on studying the role, I found that I had one line in the graveyard and that three major plot scenes took place at the Hilton. As my contract was only for two days I saw cause for alarm, though not necessarily despondency. If they thought they were going to shoot what amounted to my entire part in one day, they had another think coming.

I rang my agents and told them to inform Puck Films that the deal was off, if they really expected me to cover some twenty pages of dialogue in one day. Miss Richmond (or could it have been Mrs Richmond?) was apparently frightfully sympathetic and cooed down the machine, saying that she had the Hilton eating out of her hand, which seemed a curious way of a hotel behaving. And, she added, there was no question of rushing the scenes, and the film company had been told they could stay there indefinitely. Slightly reassured by this dispatch, I asked for a tiny bit more money, didn't get it, and went back to the Steam Room of the Turkish Bath in the RAC which is the acme of decorum, but not ideal for reading scripts in.

Fortunately the dialogue was fairly easy to learn, and a few days later, when I got my first call, Masterman, the master-mind, had mastered most of the part. I had been asked to report at the hotel at 7.30 for make-up.

'I'm not using it. I never do,' I replied, hoping to put the dreaded hour off at least half an hour. 'All the same, Mr Bull,' said the second assistant, 'we would appreciate it very much if you were there at 7.30 all the same.'

So I rose from my bed at 6.45 (there are a good many more inconvenient locations than Park Lane for a Chelsea resident), I hopped on to a bus as I hadn't succeeded in increasing my daily rate and disembarked at Hyde Park Corner. I strolled over to the angular building which has done so much to disfigure the skyline of the West One Postal District of London. My reception at Reception in the hotel was, I felt, less than cordial, and it muttered Room something or other, indicating the spacious elevators. An impertinent minion showed me how to work the damned thing and a minute later I found myself in an enormously overheated room (The Americans like it you see), and on the bed lay a large man, whom I had obviously disturbed in slumber. He turned out to be an actor, unknown to me, who was not in the best of tempers. Apparently the unit had worked until midnight, then gone on strike, announcing their intention of not returning until 10.30 at the earliest.

As usual the actors due to appear the following day had been the last to hear of the change in schedule, and certainly no-one had bothered to phone me. I didn't think it was worth going home, or indeed even having a 'French Lesson' in Curzon Street round the corner, where delightful ladies were still searching for 'apt pupils'. I decided to have a zizz there and then on the unoccupied bed of the two.

I had just got off to an uneasy slumber when I was awakened by Miss Richmond, who apologized for the muck-up and stated that there was a special room reserved as my dressing-room. She indicated that it was one of great beauty. It didn't turn out to be exactly that, but it was cooler and didn't have a large gent lying on one of the beds. What it did have lying on one of the beds was, or were, a brief-case and a bowler hat. I looked quizzically at them and then at Miss Richmond. Possibly one eyebrow raised itself an eighth of an inch.

'The Producer's,' she announced without a word of explanation and I thought it expedient to keep my trap shut. After she'd made her exit, I endeavoured to zizz again without much success. I subsequently realized that I should have followed the example of some of the less scrupulous artistes by putting through a good few continental phone calls, ordering far from continental breakfasts and charging it all to the film company.

I was called to the set just before lunch. It turned out to be a banqueting room called the 'Pompeian'. In the film it was to play a Board Room and I'm not even going to bother to make a joke about that. It was very small indeed and, once all the lights were on, claustrophobic in the extreme. To add to the discomfort the air-conditioning had to be turned off during the actual 'take' which not only caused near suffocation in the room itself, but must have infuriated the actual residents.

I knew one or two of my fellow actors, who, while we were waiting for a rehearsal, regaled me with hair-raising tales of the first week's shooting on *Licensed To Kill*. Conditions of hardship and continuous hours, which necessitated the calling in of an Actors' Equity representative, had also resulted in wives arriving to take away their semi-demented menfolk and vice-versa. Apparently the organization of the film left something to be desired, and the Hilton, already fed up to the back teeth, had demanded that everyone leave the building by 5.30 that evening and not return.

I took another gander at my script and realized that there was no chance of getting through more than one of the three scenes scheduled to be filmed in that hotel. I approached the harassed director who looked as if he hadn't slept at all during the week and probably hadn't. He informed me that he might have to cut the second scene, a decision he would deplore, he said. As a matter of fact I thought it'd be a pity too, as it was the only scene in which I had the resemblance of a funny line.

Just before breaking for lunch, we managed to get a 'master' shot of the first scene into the can. A 'master' is a long 'take' in which the whole scene is usually shot from some distance and without any close-ups. At least I *think* that's what it means, and it may be of no help to you.

After that the unit went off to feed and I decided to retire to my room, as I was now getting seriously alarmed by the amount of stuff we might be forced to shoot before packing up. I am absolutely hopeless when working under pressure; frogs get into my throat, words come out sideways, and the total result is appalling; and on this occasion I was nearing 'panic stations'.

After lunch there was nothing to allay my misgivings. The producer, a Mr Ward, had recovered his hat and briefcase but they didn't seem to have inspired him with much confidence as he stood about gloomily surveying the scene. My stand-in (his name was Steve Donoghue. No, not the riding gentleman, sillies!) asked me if I fancied anything to eat. This is the sort of thing good stand-ins tend to do and it raises the morale considerably. I said I wouldn't half mind an apple. A short time later a diminutive page arrived with a whole basket of fruit. The resourceful Mr Donoghue asked one of the assistants to sign the bill which he surprisingly did, and I started distributing largesse as if I were Mr Laurence Harvey dishing out the special wine with which he is apt to travel.

We completed the first scene scheduled in a fairly haphazard way by about three-thirty. There were two hours left to shoot a frightfully complicated scene, for which those stalwarts of the industry, the Messrs Felix Felton, sadly and recently deceased, and Francis de Woolf had arrived some five hours previously. But instead of embarking on this, Mr Shonteff, our director, decided to shoot the film in sequence and that the scene he had just decided to discard, would be the next on the agenda after all. As things were already pretty tense the question of the third scene was not discussed, although Mr Felton and Mr de Woolf were told that they could leave the building. Mr Ward and Miss Richmond could be observed deep in excited conclave in various corners of the hotel, while Mr Billy Milton and I polished off our scene in the Pompeian Room, and I even timed the Joke fairly accurately.

I know you've all been dying to know what the Joke was and I shall jolly well tell you though it'll fall as flat as a pancake, out of context. Coming on top of a series of murders I'd either committed or caused to be committed, I said to my henchman,

'By the way, Wilson, never say die!' Frightfully funny what!

At five o'clock we were told that we could all go. There was no doubt that the instructions came rather from the Hilton than Puck Films. I pottered over to Mr Shonteff.

'What about the other scene?' I asked him, suspecting that he, as part author and director, must know that a large section of the plot was contained in this portion of the script.

'We'll have to do it somewhere else. I thought the British Museum might be a good idea,' he said vaguely. I decided there wasn't much future in asking him *when* this was likely to happen, but I did see Miss Richmond as I was about to pass into the night.

She smiled benignly at me like, I imagine, Her Majesty the Queen might, after arranging a particularly successful Royal Tea Party.

'And when can you come again?' she asked as if inviting me to a series of rather expensive lectures on 'How to Stop Smoking by Hypnotism'. I told her that any day before 3 April would suit me fine as on that date I was leaving for Greece. It was then 12 March, and would, I thought, have afforded Puck Films ample time to rearrange their schedule accordingly. Miss Richmond reacted to my information as if it was the Worst National Disaster since Bobby Moore was nearly arrested for not stealing a bracelet on the eve of the World Cup. She consulted a notebook.

'But every day *up* to 3 April is fully booked for other scenes. We couldn't possibly fit it in before then,' she announced.

I smiled sweetly, shrugged my shoulders, and hurried out of the building. Rather too hurriedly, as it turned out, as I left with Mr Felix Felton's overcoat. My only excuse was that the atmosphere of the Pompeian Room and the feeling of utter despair at having said I'd do the film in the first place, had unhinged me.

I hadn't even tried on the coat for size as it was a steaming hot spring day, and I bundled it and myself into a taximeter cabriolet and went bowling home in a state of near collapse. Later the blower went and it was Mr Felton telling me that he had my overcoat, which, though he gallantly admitted was in a slightly better condition than his own, would not fit him. It was too small apparently, a fact which, while boosting my morale, gave me a keener sense of guilt as it's always better to wear clothes too large for one than vice-versa. The coats' owners discussed the likelihood of their scene ever being shot and decided unanimously that it would be safer to change overcoats irrespective of the machinations of Puck Films.

It turned out that Mr Felton, who resided in Herts., had to come up to town the following Monday and where by chance would I be that p.m.? By chance I reported that I would be around the Cambridge Circus area, doing a test Voice Over for Frozen Peas. I suggested a meeting and Mr F. concurred.

On the day scheduled for the Great Overcoat Handover there was a surprisingly violent thunderstorm as I alighted from my omnibus in Shaftesbury Avenue.

I therefore had to make use of Mr Felton's property and my guilt complex increased at the thought of having to hand over to him not only a purloined but sodden garment.

In the recording studio I found a third largish gentleman waiting. This turned out to be my old friend Paul Whitsun-Jones. We are sometimes competitors for the same jobs, but as he has numerous accomplishments that I don't possess, like singing in tune for example, he usually gets the role.

Anyhow, there was Paul studying his lines for his part or, as I had thought up to that moment, my part. We greeted each other boisterously and suddenly I thought of Mr Felton's approach. I started to laugh and told Paul why.

'What! Old Fish Fingers!' he exclaimed, 'Oh lawks, I hope they don't nab him instead of one of us. Can't you give him the coat in the street?'

It turned out that Mr Felton was one of the 'Voices Over' most in demand for commercial advertising in the business. But, perhaps fortunately for both of us, he didn't turn up owing to the inclemency of the weather, and so I was able to dry his overcoat in time for the actual handover, which took place in the Aquarium at the Zoo, you won't be surprised to hear, for that was the spot in which Puck Films finally decided to film our joint scene.

Curiously enough, years later, the mantle, but not the overcoat, of Old Fish Fingers was to descend on me. And I was not only 'Voice Over' but 'Face Over' which is not nearly as chic as being Heard and not Seen. But more of that anon, though not, I suspect, in this chapter. Let's get back to Puck Films, a far less profitable source of employment as it turned out. Now where were we? Oh yes, leaving the Hilton Hotel in a certain amount of confusion.

My next call from the unit had as a location the most macabre I have had in my 'Forty Years in the Film Industry', as my next vol. of reminiscences is almost certainly not going to be called.

'Would I be at the office,' the second assistant enquired, 'at such and such a time so as to be driven to Golders Green crematorium for the funeral scene?' It appeared that Graveyards were out as a location. I started out for the suite off the Edgware Road fairly cheerfully, as it was intimated in my script that I would only have to say, 'Everything has gone according to plan, Miss.' (Veronica Hurst as it turned out.) It was a line that even I thought I might be able to get out, if pressed. I was to be disguised as an undertaker (you may or may not remember that I was playing Masterman the Master Mind or something or other who was trying to do something beastly to twin scientists played by Karel Stepanek).

As the film company did not seem to possess in their Wardrobe Department an appropriate costume, I had to wrest from the moths a morning suit I had worn thirty years previously, when called on to play a long series of butlers at the Coventry Repertory Theatre. It is curious that neither the Butlers' or Undertakers' Rig of the day appear to have changed in three decades, but I think that even my old suit was deeply shocked on its resurrection day.

One of the repellent features of the occasion was that there was more genuine opportunity for jokes in Bad Taste than can have occurred in any film in the history of the cinema. You can just imagine how any irreverent body of people, like a film unit, would be so embarrassed by the circs. that they'll stoop to anything. I know I did by starting the day off with a series of wildly unsuitable cracks. It was bitterly cold and by the evening we were all frozen by both the weather conditions and the atmosphere in the Hall of Memory as we stood or sat about unhappy and silent.

A great many of us have been shocked, though shiveringly amused, by the American Way of Death, as depicted by Mr Evelyn Waugh and Miss Jessica Mitford, but the British Way of Ditto seemed to me, on this showing, almost equally hypocritical, and in a way more sinister. I don't know the actual financial details of the deal by which Puck Films were enabled to lease the Hall of Memory for the day, but it surely cannot have been for the publicity. Judging by the Crematorium Call-Sheet for the day, which I managed to get hold of, there simply didn't seem to be a vacant moment during it when the coffins weren't being whirred in, and urns whirred out. Quite often there was only ten minutes between the services, though of course there are several chapels at Golders Green.

Knowing the enormous and understandable desire on the part of Puck Films to keep expenses down, it must have been a cheaper proposition to lease the Hall of Memory for the day, rather than find (a) some churchyard or (b) a tiny studio where the scene could have been shot quite simply. As it was, the Crematorium authorities had to interrupt their daily routine to quite a notable extent, which upset quite a few of what can only be described as 'customers'.

The ordinary cremations, it must be admitted, continued to take place throughout the day and there were fourteen on the schedule. But the people who had journeyed from far afield to visit the Hall of Memory arrived to be told that it was closed that day to the general public. It must have been deeply distasteful to these pilgrims who had come to pay their respects to the remains of their Loved Ones, to see instead a lot of actors in make-up around a make-believe coffin. The latter was incidentally the one used for rehearsal of the State Funeral of Sir Winston Churchill, a fact which sent Miss Richmond, our Production lady, into paroxysms of excitement. She phoned the Publicity Dept. immediately in order to inform them of their luscious bit of luck in securing this sensational bonne bouche.

I'm surprised Puck Films didn't include in their script some of the riveting info. contained in the daily call sheet, issued by the Crematorium to its employees. The deceased were all numbered and they had reached 180959, I don't mind telling you. At the side of each service was the time scheduled, the name of the firm in charge of the 'arrangements', the name of the deceased and that of the cleric presiding over the service. The last column was devoted to notes on special effects, particularly for the musical department. 'Sheep May Safely Graze' was to be played at 12.10, but in a service for a Humanist on the agenda there were instructions that no funeral music or 'Jerusalem' was to be played. Three pews were to be reserved and 'a large crowd' was expected. There was to be 'no incense' for a Mr Ali Khan, and a coffin of somebody else was apparently 'zinc lined'. In one case the coffin was to precede the mourners and in another, 'Air on a G String' had been chosen as Exit music. 'We'll gather Lilacs' was to be played at 3.30 as entrance music and at 3.40 for exit music.

Hmmmm. 'We'll gather Lilacs.' Just outside the Hall of Memory there is a plaque to Ivor Novello the author-composer of this immensely popular tune and a rose tree is planted nearby to perpetuate his name. I had plenty of time during the long day to wander around and all sorts of fascinating details caught my attention. In the Hall of Memory itself are a series of small flower vases, full of fresh flowers, obviously tributes to those recently deceased. On the upper floors are countless caskets decorated with artificial flowers and/or photographs (I even saw snaps of dogs and cats alongside the urns). Many famous names are in evidence, including Anna Pavlova, who left instructions that white flowers should always bower her remains.

At the entrance there is a sort of catalogue of Services to the Public. You can pay a certain sum to have the name of the deceased entered into the Golden Book of Memory; there are scaled charges for flowers to be placed in the vases and the various forms of services with or without organs, choirs, etc. I wondered if those paying for cremations on that particular day would get a reduction, owing to the presence of the film unit all over the place.

The mere sight of the Sound vans, equipment and various actors smoking like chimneys, while smoke emanating from mortal remains was going up through them, was more than worrying to me. Yet if we had all walked about as if at a funeral (actual) it might have been even more reprehensible. I do know that most of us spent an acutely disquieting day and in the early evening I caught sight of one of the younger and seemingly more cynical members of the cast, sitting quietly in a Non-Smoking pew reading the Bible.

'There will be a letter or two about this in the papers,' I thought to myself. And indeed there apparently were, written by some of the sad people who had journeyed to the Crematorium in vain. They had found the Hall of Memory Out of Bounds as if it were a war-time café. I should think and hope that Puck Films will be the last film company allowed to make use of the place during working hours. At one minute I was silly enough to ask why in Heaven's name weren't we shooting this particular sequence at night? Ask a silly question and you get a silly answer. The overtime involved would have been prohibitive.

As far as I was concerned professionally, my first and only shot was completed just after eleven in the morning, but Mr Shonteff indicated that he might want me for a close-up later in the day, and would I mind hanging around. I did just this until seven in the evening when I was told I could go. By this time I was in a distinct huff and Flounced Out. Miss Richmond, ever watchful, ran after me and asked if I was upset. I just glared at her. She then observed, rather endearingly I thought, that she doubted if I would want to work for Puck Films again. She said Mr Ward would be most distressed when she told him how unhappy I was and would I like to have his chauffeur drive me home. I accepted with alacrity, forgetting that as the Crematorium was considered 'location' they would have to get me home somehow.

I still had my big scene to play and I waited agog to hear where that was going to be shot. Inside the gas chambers of Belsen perhaps? No, it turned out to be the Aquarium at the Zoo and it was planned for 1 April, an admirable choice you will agree. You must remember that the scene was *meant* to be shot in the Hilton Hotel so it was really quite a switch. In a way it was the most sensational of the three days in which I was to create the part of Masterman the Master Mind, and I still cannot believe that any of the incidents on this particular April Fool's Day ever took place.

There were three actors involved in the scene. Mr Felton, Mr de Woolf and myself. I took an early opportunity of returning to the former his long overdue overcoat. But I could see no sign of Mr de Woolf. I discovered that he'd caught a severe chill at Golders Green Crematorium and was seriously ill as a result, and there was no chance of him completing his role in the film. As time was precious, Puck Films decided to shoot 'round him' and had engaged a similarly bearded man to represent him. Unfortunately this particular artiste had not shown up on the morning specified so the make-up man had had to practise his art on a member of the unit, who in my humble opinion, looked quite fascinatingly unlike Mr de Woolf and I didn't see how anyone of the film's prospective customers, unless completely blind, could be deceived. The plot was quite confusing enough without further hazards of this kind. However, the director, camera gentlemen, first assistant and Miss Richmond went about their business completely unperturbed and apparently the whole of this key scene was to be shot either at the backs of, or over our heads.

It must be confessed that the Aquarium was very dark indeed inside and this fact would help the director and cameramen to weave their magic. The authorities had not suspended their business and school parties, foreign visitors and the general public came through to watch the great turtles and other vast denizens of the deep.

'Not very good specimens. Too fat,' said a cavilling lady as she gave a passing glance of disfavour at Mr Felton and myself.

It appeared to be a popular day for making films at the Zoo as there were two other units working there. At the Monkey House nearby, Woodfall Films had set up shop and were shooting *Morgan. A Suitable Case for Treatment.* As most of this lot had worked with me on *Tom Jones* it provided a welcome respite from conditions in and around the Aquarium. Also I was able to steal quite a lot of goodies from their mobile canteen, which not unnaturally had a greater variety than that provided by Puck Films! Though it must be admitted that on this particularly balmy morning I do remember the ever resourceful Miss Richmond dishing out bangers to all and sundry which she was bemustarding herself. Later on in the day I was to hear from various members of the unit of the traumas which had accompanied the shooting of the film since Crematorium Day. There had been a complete sit-down strike at Burnham Beeches (of all places) when Miss Richmond had apparently unwisely referred to some of the unit as 'the scum of the industry', which hadn't gone down all that well. So, as they were now nearing the end of the film, the banger orgy was probably part of a conciliatory campaign.

Anyhow there seemed relative calm in the Aquarium, and, bored with it, I wandered back to the *Morgan* lot, where I tried to edge myself into a scene with David Warner. This young performer had made his film debut being tutored by Mr John Moffatt and myself in the bioscope *Tom Jones.* During a final rehearsal I crept out of a Zoo phone box, where I had been hiding, and glided into position beside him without his noticing. However, the director Mr Karel Reisz, while thanking me for my willingness to help, thought that my sudden appearance in the film might jeopardize its chances with less sophisticated audiences. So I slunk back to the Aquarium as the third film unit, currently using the establishment's facilities, were by now on the Mappin Terraces and I could see no furtherment of my career by chasing *them* across the mountainous terrain.

On my return to the unit I learned that there was to be no shooting before lunch, which we had in the Zoo Restaurant. People appeared to stare at us in far more amazement than they had viewed the Boa Constrictors or the Unfriendly Vulture. I suppose we didn't look like anything on earth. Certainly not people making a film.

After the repast we actually shot the scene. It was macabre because without the physical presence of one of the principal actors, Mr de Woolf, it was impossible to believe that the scene would actually appear on the screen. It all felt like an exercise at a Dramatic School (First Term).

We were driven back to the Puck Film offices off the Edgware Road in a Rolls Royce, which had been engaged to play in the movie and was also on a higher daily rate than any of us, I fancy. It was the first touch of luxury I had enjoyed during the entire shooting of the film (every bit of three days but it seemed like three years). Felix and I lolled back and enjoyed ourselves hugely, snugly wrapped up in our own overcoats for a change.

Back in the bedroom which formed a major part of the film company's office, Karel Stepanek, our star, was lying down trying to relax. He was in for some night shooting and had seemingly been hanging about all day. There were suddenly about ten people in the room, including half the unit who were going off to shoot some exteriors of the Hilton. No-one was keen on letting us back *inside* the hotel I don't mind telling you. Anyhow the scene was strongly reminiscent of the crowded cabin in *A Night at the Opera* with the Marx Brothers. Felix and I were taking up a bit of space as we were waiting to do some post-syncing of the stuff we had just shot in the Aquarium. Owing to the de Woolf hang up I *did* see that a certain amount of ingenuity would have to be used to make the scene real. It was bedlam in the offices and quite suddenly Mr Stepanek blew his top and who could blame him? After a superb tirade of abuse against the company about its treatment of artistes, he left the building. Miss Richmond turned on the first assistant who turned on the second and so on.

In order to ease the situation I announced to anyone who was listening that Mr Felton and I would be throwing our respective temperaments in a matter of moments unless immediate steps were taken which would enable us to complete our assignment.

There was a brief hush and we were shepherded away to a curious flat in the same building as the offices. It apparently belonged to our producer Mr Ward, and was a very suitable place to do our post-syncing in as it looked the most unlived in apartment I've ever cracked my peepers on. Mr Felton and I, with the help of the sound gentleman, said our lines over and over again in a variety of ways and with totally similar intonations and went away quietly and soberly.

That's the last I heard of Puck Films. I never saw *Licensed to Kill*, but as is always the case with work of which one is thoroughly ashamed, everyone else did. It was called *The Second Best Secret Agent in the Whole Wide World* in the States and elsewhere and cleaned up I'm told. Influential people saw it and were flabbergasted. My friends just didn't believe it but the staff of the Greek Bank which I patronized adored it and gave me their version of the plot.

III

LIFE IS A CUCUMBER IN AMERICA

7. *The Dickens of a Mess (U.S. Style)*

I DON'T think I have ever been classed as a 'difficult' actor, mainly because I've always been certain that directors, producers, and a large percentage of my fellow artistes know far more about the business than I do. Consequently I'll put up with any amount of criticism if it seems justified but on the rare occasions when someone really gets on my wick, I have to fight back, because I cannot bear injustice in any shape or form. The only recent encounter of this type I've experienced was a faint feud which hardly rippled the waters of Broadway, but it was with one of its most powerful inhabitants, viz, as my father used to say, the impresario David Merrick.

I would like to point out at the outset that I have enormous admiration for him on several levels and that as a showman he has few peers. He has been instrumental in introducing shows and actors to America which wouldn't otherwise have seen the light of day there and I think he is a genuine enthusiast of the theatre. It's just that he doesn't like actors and knows nothing about them, and that I think is a failing in one whose business is the theatre and whose reputation and living depend on the artistes saying the right words at the right time in the right place.

I had had previous experience of him with the great monk musical *Luther* and personally had little cause for complaint during that happy engagement. When he kindly engaged me for *Pickwick* in America, I was delighted as my salary had risen for this entertainment. I know that it was entirely due to Harry Secombe, the star, and Peter Coe, the director, that I was offered the job in the first place and allowed to join the company rather late in its pre-Broadway tour, but it was nice of Mr Merrick to allow them to have their way (in this instance).

The history of his affair with *Pickwick* was a curious one and I am still not absolutely certain of the facts. It is believed that he bought it after it opened in Manchester, as a result of the vast amount of money he had made on *Oliver*. Then his interest faded and, though I am not sure if he ever saw the London production, he allowed the option to lapse. Then, on learning of its huge and lasting success at the Saville Theatre, he started negotiations again. I think it is fairly obvious that he never liked it much himself, because that is the only possible excuse for his subsequent extraordinary behaviour.

Pickwick's American run started in San Francisco in the spring of 1965 to a sell-out season, largely subscribed before opening. The figures were staggering and equalled those in Los Angeles, whither it moved for a further extended run. The critics weren't wild about it, but they weren't in London either, yet the show had something for the ordinary audience which was inescapable and above all it had Harry Secombe.

Anyhow, by the time I joined it in August in Cleveland, it had nearly, if not entirely, paid off its production costs. As all the Sean Kenny sets and the costumes had been imported from England, it was nowhere near as astronomically expensive as your average new American musical.

I had been incredibly fortunate in my association with *Pickwick* in England. I had originally been asked to play a singing role in the piece, and, despite all protestations, was finally asked to do an audition. I arrived with my copy of

'Love Will Find A Way' from *The Maid of the Mountains*, my rendering of which is calculated to send even the cleaners screaming from the theatre. But instead of having to put the auditors through the ordeal, Peter Coe, the director, handed me the part of Sgt Buzfuz to have a look at, which I did, and was thrilled. Although I knew that everyone from Sir Henry Irving to Sir Donald Wolfit had played the part, somehow it did not seem so intimidating in a musical. The only trouble was that I had to leave shortly for America to play in *Luther*, and I was amazed and delighted when they agreed to release me for this. It meant four weeks in Manchester and six in London. It was a madly happy time because of the unique personality of Harry Secombe, who contrived to make every moment a party whether on or off the stage, I, in common with the rest of the company, worshipped him.

So I arrived in Cleveland full of hope and confidence, only to experience one of my worst weeks since the second one at the Anzio beach-head. It had been raining in the city and the stage door seemed knee-deep in water, or it may have been the result of the ice-machine which nightly froze the skating scene in the play. Anyway, that was my first sight of *Pickwick* in America; I then managed to locate some of the company and listen to their sagas of the tour. Apparently Cleveland was the first setback. Business not good, a very old-fashioned and dirty theatre (the Hanna), and a great deal of rehearsing. Roy Castle had arrived and was just about to take over from young Davy Jones, destined to be a 'Monkee' for a wildly successful television series.

I was taking over from the gentleman who had followed me in London and who was naturally not very pleased at relinquishing the role before the show reached New York. I got the feeling that the American members of the company, who outnumbered the British contingent by about six to one, resented my advent and considered that my predecessor had had a raw deal. But in fact he had known from the beginning that this was going to happen. However, the rest of the imported cast were warm and welcoming though I knew that I did not have to prove anything to them. But I sensed that winning over the Americans was going to be a tough assignment.

Harry was his usual enchanting self and some of the only remotely happy moments I had in Cleveland were swimming with him and his delightful family at the Motel where they were staying. Another bastion of support was Julian Orchard, who played Mr Snodgrass so beautifully. Tall, cultured and incisive, with impeccable timing, he is rapidly becoming a great favourite on TV. One of the few good things which came out of the *Pickwick* tour was his meeting and falling in love with the assistant choreographer, Suzanne France, who is almost as tall as he is. She has exquisite features and colouring, two of the most persuasive legs in the business, and now a small cheerful son called Christopher. It was Julian, by the way, who made backstage cabaret history when he was accompanying Mr Robert Morley on the first night of the latter's historic season at the Café de Paris, by having to drop some keys down Mr Morley's back to cure a nosebleed only a few minutes before they were due to go on stage.

I arrived in Cleveland on a Monday evening and Roy and I were to open on the Friday following. This left us two performances on the Saturday to settle down in, before pressing on for a month in Detroit, our penultimate stop before Broadway. As my role was what is known as a 'tear off' and lasted ten minutes, I didn't get many rehearsals, and was only permitted one bash in the set, and even that was without props because, owing to the bizarre and alarming union laws in America, if I used so much as one tiny piece of paper belonging to the set, every stage hand would have to be called for the rehearsal, and would have been paid double time at that!

So you can imagine how terrifying my opening night was. I ranted and roared my way through the part and, I gather, frightened the daylights out of the cast, but hardly got a laugh, and it is meant to be one of the great comedy parts of our time. The next day I relaxed a bit, and even more when I learned that my predecessor was leaving the environs.

At Detroit, Julian and I clocked into a hotel called the Lexington. It had several advantages; it was near the theatre and had a waitress doubling on the violin in the evening. In the early morning when she served us breakfast, we thought our tired old eyes were deceiving us, but not a bit of it. Our eyes were tired mainly because it was in Detroit that Mr Merrick decided to pep the show up a bit and sheets and sheets of new material were thrown at us daily.

Now the principal asset of *Pickwick* was that it worked as a framework for the superbly comic and inventive performance of Harry Secombe, of whom I am sure the original author would have approved. Apart from that, it had an innate corniness, some hummable tunes (including the much played 'If I Ruled the World') and some very ingenious sets by Sean Kenney which moved round in circles and as usual provided a dangerous hazard for the unwary actor. Because the reaction in Cleveland and Detroit was not strong for the book, our producer decided to infuse some hot numbers and endeavour to remove anything remotely Dickensian.

The trial scene, for instance, which was almost verbatim the author's work, Mr Merrick really hated. I was asked to cut as much off as possible and he still thought it plain and dull. 'Is the Trial Scene getting any more laughs?' he used to hiss as he lurked under the stage at the Fisher Theater, Detroit. 'I don't *think* so,' I used to say with a sad but sweet smile.

As it was the only scene I was in, I was fairly desperate not to have it changed; it had worked in London and I saw no reason why it shouldn't in New York. They might not laugh at it 'in the sticks', but it provided the only real drama for the character of Pickwick in the play. And Mrs Bardell's breach of promise case is fairly famous in the annals of literature so you can imagine my consternation when Peter Coe handed me an entirely new Trial Scene which contained not one single line of the original text.

This particular event took place in Mr Secombe's dressing-room after a performance. He was present and so was the author of the new script. His name was Sidney Michaels and he had adapted *Chin Chin* from the French and the *Life of Dylan Thomas.* He was now in the process of adapting *Pickwick.*

Peter had handed me the pieces of paper with the words 'Sidney wants you to read this.' 'Oh, how nice,' I had said, beaming at the playwright. After I had studied it, I said, 'Very interesting. What is it?' Peter Coe informed me that it was a New Trial Scene. I asked who was going to play it. I then had the gall to ask Mr Michaels if he had ever actually read *The Pickwick Papers,* and he had the bravery, but impertinence, to say that he had not. As he had been under contract to Mr Merrick for several weeks on this assignment it seemed a curious confession.

What I disliked most about the scene Mr Michaels had written was that while omitting all the famous lines like 'Chops *and* tomato sauce!', he had paraphrased the entire original and you can guess what that was like.

It was the first of several Trial Scenes presented to me via Mr Coe and I did make clear that I would rather leave the building than not speak the original stuff, which I had already cut dangerously near the bone. My predecessor was available I thought and I would be only too glad to make way for him under the circumstances. Harry Secombe protected me and boosted my morale though he himself was suffering from agonizing gout. It was a ghastly time altogether. Roy Castle and Anton Rodgers worked like fury on new numbers and so did the rest of the cast, only to find them dropped a few performances after they'd put them in the show. Added to all this our talented choreographer Gillian Lynne and Peter Coe did not see exactly eye to eye and the whole show began to disintegrate.

Some of the company, particularly the American element,

thought that any change was for the better and as we got nearer Broadway things got worse and worse. But it must be remembered that when *Hello Dolly* opened at the same theatre in Detroit it got very indifferent notices, and some of the chorus started angling for other jobs. And we all know what happened to that show.

My Trial Scene remained the same, but my actual trials were not yet over. We started rehearsing a new scene in which, for some inexplicable reason, Sgt Buzfuz was made an Election candidate standing against Mr Pickwick. The company marched round the stage singing an incomprehensible lyric and I sulked on a supposed balcony muttering my few lines without the slightest conviction. It absolutely ruined my sudden appearance in the Court Scene and I genuinely thought it was gravely detrimental to the play. This insertion was dropped and I breathed again.

There was, however, a lovely Woolworths in Detroit, and thither hied Julian Orchard and myself whenever we could. It was the only branch I had come across which had myna birds in the basement and a lady on the ground floor encouraging electric organ buyers and teaching them to play by numbers. I was in there on my own one day when I saw Julian approaching.

'Please,' I said to the lady on the organ, 'play "Ain't Misbehavin'" for this gentleman as he's thinking of buying your instrument.' I then vanished into the basement to listen to the myna birds screeching at the religious pictures.

And talking of that sort of thing, one of my crosses in the show was a greatly talented but not overdisciplined actress, whom I will call for various reasons Charlotte Rae. She had, I was assured on unimpeachable authority, started off in San Francisco superb in the role and looking exactly like the Phiz drawing. However, during the tour, she dropped the heavy make-up, tarted up her hair, and emerged as a shortish, but handsome Jewish lady, which I am sure was not quite what Charles Dickens had in mind when he created the character of Mrs Bardell.

She also came over very strongly indeed. Poor Harry had to bear the brunt of it, and in the love scene she came near to stifling him once or twice with her elaborate caresses. Mistress of the Understatement, she certainly was not. In the Trial Scene, instead of remaining silent and helpless, as Jessie Evans had so beautifully done in the London production, she suddenly sprang up and started making faces or exclamations whenever I opened my mouth, which was frequently in this short scene. Finally I told the director that it had gone far enough and I couldn't take any more, so we had another Detroit confrontation scene, this time in Miss Rae's dressing-room.

'Oh but Peter,' she remonstrated, 'you're so wonderful in the part that I've had to rethink it all over again, and I feel that I ought to react to everything you say.'

'Surely not *everything*, Charlotte?' I replied.

She promised to tone it all down a bit. Her husband, a musician who was travelling with us, was very busy writing new songs for the show. Actually, he wrote one for his wife which was charming, and got into the show. It was called 'Mrs Bardell has a Room to Let' and she sang it early on in the entertainment.

One night I arrived half-way through the show as was my wont, not being required to make my first appearance much before ten thirty of an evening and four thirty of an afternoon, and the long suffering Bill Dodds, our stage director, warned me to expect a slight change in the court scene. My eyes narrowed (if that is possible).

'Oh yes,' I said, 'and what *might* I expect?'

'Well,' explained Mr Dodds hesitantly, 'Charlotte is going to sing a few bars from "Mrs Bardell has a Room to Let" when she takes the witness stand.'

At the beginning of the Trial, as I opened my trap, I was conscious of hearing the vast orchestra sorting out their music as if they were about to embark on the whole of *Götterdämmerung*. Suddenly, Mrs Bardell, who was in theory so faint from terror that I was supposed to support her to the witness stand, began to sing. I stood, arms akimbo, watching her open-mouthed; apparently I was supposed to stop her, but I didn't. She went on and on and on, and I'm afraid that the pro-Bull faction of the crowd tittered. After the scene Miss Rae reprimanded me for not interrupting her after a few bars.

'But Charlotte, it was so charming!' I found myself saying.

And *that* didn't happen again I am happy to say, but Detroit was a trying time in every sense of the word. When Harry had gout, a happy extrovert called Taylor Reed played the part, and did not appear to have a nerve in his head. The Detroit audiences, who hadn't caught Harry at it, didn't notice the difference, but goodness, *we* did.

It was very hot weather, which didn't help much, and I was lucky in being able to spend any free time I had at the Detroit Yachting Club, where everyone seemed very rich, much against integration, and talked mainly about motor cars. And why the hell shouldn't they? At least it was more interesting than the traumatic situations at the Fisher Theater.

Like all good times, bad times come to an end too, and eventually we pressed on to Washington, our final touring date. I hadn't been there since I had played in Christopher Fry's *The Lady's not for Burning* in 1950 and I was much looking forward to a return visit. I was not disappointed. I had dear friends there who had a praying mantis in their garden, and Julian and I shacked up in one of the nicest hotels I have ever stayed in. It was called the Jefferson and was slightly above our station as regards cost, but well worth it. Every room was decorated entirely differently, with great taste and originality.

The National Theater, where we played, was a reasonable size and the audiences were quite enthusiastic for a change. Mrs Merrick attended our opening there which was more helpful, I think, than her husband would have been, whom she left shortly afterwards. Attempts were made to put in a couple of new numbers but after our first week there the show was more or less 'frozen' and we returned to New York on a train, which made a change. We were to open at the Forty-Sixth Street Theater, a new building with a continuously sloping auditorium and not quite enough dressing-rooms. Except for the cast of *I Do I Do* which played there shortly afterwards and had a huge cast of two—Mary Martin and Robert Preston.

We were to have several previews and two dress rehearsals and during this period a series of new dramas took place. Possibly as a result of Mr Merrick's refusing to send for Sean Kenny to set up his intricate scenery for reasons of expenses, a piece of scenery fell from 'the flies' and nearly caused a serious accident. Our producer departed with Miss Mary Martin and *Hello Dolly* to Vietnam in a blaze of publicity just before our opening. Possibly a wise decision. Bill Dodds got a stone in his kidney, just before opening night, and his extremely efficient assistant Peter Stern got us through with a technically perfect performance which was a miracle.

I went through the first night in a sort of daze and stayed in my friend Frith Banbury's room in the Piccadilly Hotel opposite until the last possible moment. The audience was as tough as old boots but it had never been a show to send the sophisticates wild with delight. I did not go to the Merrick-subsidized party afterwards, but sneaked off to spend the rest of the evening with loving friends.

To cap it all, there was a newspaper strike on, although opinions were divided whether or not this was a Good Thing under the circumstances. However there was one rave on the TV and most of the radio reviews were quite enthusiastic. I did get to see the notice which *should* have appeared in the *New York Times*, and I doubt whether it would have done us much good. I collected a dream review in *Time* magazine which said that: 'In all this tedious mishmash, only Peter Bull as Sergeant Buzfuz shows an authentic Dickensian flair. Like a Daumier-lawyer print brought to life, he knows the precise satirical boiling point where caricature reveals character, where broadness of humour acquires the beef of wit. He is an estimable and melancholy measure of the show that might have been.'

I only wish I could have seen Mr Merrick's face when he read that. I never saw our producer again, but after we had closed abruptly under circumstances which I will explain shortly, I stayed on in New York doing television appearances and preparing a diatribe about my ex-employer in order to vindicate our beloved star from any possible implication that the seeming failure of the show had anything to do with him. He was, I think, treated disgracefully as were the rest of the company and the only way I could think of to express my feelings was to write a letter to the Editor of *Variety*, who printed it in toto which surprised me, under the heading: 'Actor raps closing of *Pickwick*, and Chilly Treatment of Talent.'

'Dear Sir,

A small item in the show obituary column of *Variety* recently caught my eye. It read *Pickwick* folded after fifty-six performances at an approximate break-even or perhaps a small profit, as a personal investment for the producer, David Merrick.

'I wonder how many eyebrows were raised at this announcement, and I hope that some of the backers of the show, to say nothing of the members of the public who actually enjoyed the entertainment, will be as surprised at the sudden withdrawal of *Pickwick* as most of the acting profession appears to be. Was it not fairly common knowledge around Broadway that, in spite of rough critical handling and a shaky start, it played to around $50,000 a week? Was it not agreed that most, if not all, of its production costs were paid off on the road? And, above all, was it not maintained by the most sceptical people that it would clean up at Christmas, to say nothing of Thanksgiving?

'Indeed special matinées and prices were being quoted in the press until a few days of its closing. At the last matinée (Standing Room Only as were most matinées) the theatre was packed with children, who not only gave the cast the most astounding ovation after the show, but crowded round the stage door afterwards to ask why *Pickwick* was being withdrawn. A good question, as it happened to be the ideal Christmas fare, with its jolly unsexy knockabout fun, real ice-skating and riveting changes of scene.

'I am no clairvoyant, but I would hazard a guess that the backers and indeed Merrick himself would have reaped a rich reward eventually, if he had not seemingly lost complete interest in the enterprise. It is certain that the sight of angry mums and gritty children demanding refunds would have been avoided in Thanksgiving week.*

'Merrick will point out that the advance was small. And this is indubitably a fact, but the size of the advance was probably due (a) to the almost negligible publicity for the show after the first few weeks, and (b) the curious behaviour of the gents in the box office, who were refusing, presumably on orders from someone, to take any telephone bookings on the grounds that the theatre was sold out on any future date that a customer was requiring seats for. This bewildered the poor old general public as well it might, for they had read in the papers that seats were available as far ahead as New Year's Eve.

'Merrick will doubtless point out to his angels that the operating "nut" for *Pickwick* was high. Again absolutely true, but will he tell them that no effort was made to cut it before posting the closing notice? The only suggestion for a cut in the size of the chorus was made after the opening performance.

'The star of *Pickwick*, Mr Harry Secombe, was powerless to make any suggestion (a) because he was ill with mumps when the decision to close the show was reached and (b) because Mr Merrick did not speak to him from a few days before the opening until after the closing date

* Usually the last week in November.

had been settled. Secombe got his notice on the day before he was due to return to the show. It arrived at his hotel delivered by a third person.

'Now Mr Secombe, who is not only the biggest musical star in England but also far and away the most loved and respected member of the theatrical profession there, is, I submit, entitled at any rate to a show of good manners, however insincere, from any impresario who, on the first night (in absentia) sent a message which read "I am proud and privileged to present you in your first New York appearance."

'Another star from England, Roy Castle, made a big personal success in the show and his experience was even more impersonal. Merrick did not speak to him from the day he opened until—well, he hasn't spoken to him yet.

'"Actors are children" Merrick keeps on saying, but surely even he must realize that children must be spoken to once in a while. But I fear the Personal Touch, which has successfully and beneficially been a feature of the theatrical world for so long, is vanishing from the business.

'My own theory about Merrick's conduct of this particular production is that he never really liked *Pickwick*. He certainly didn't take up his option after seeing it in England. His renewed interest was only kindled after seeing the big profit it was making in London. He lost it again when his sweeping structural alterations did not work out in Detroit and Washington.

'His approach to "improving" the show during this period was arbitrary and I think just a tiny bit irresponsible. It was particularly curious as Merrick had allowed the show to play for three months to enormous grosses on the West Coast with hardly any alterations. But after the pre-Broadway shake-up, the older members of the company were alarmed by the lack of faith in the original merits of the show.

'On reaching the Promised Land, in this case Broadway, *Pickwick* played a few moderately successful previews and

Merrick, perhaps wisely, disappeared to Vietnam to give Mr Cabot Lodge a severe drubbing for not inviting the chorus of *Hello Dolly* to "chow" with the stars. It is interesting to note the producer's sudden concern for the lower theatrical strata as it only seems yesterday (actually 1963) when I, as a principal in his production of *Luther*, had to decline his offer of supper after the first night, because he had omitted, doubtless in error, to invite the entire cast.

'Anyhow, his absence around the opening of *Pickwick* passed almost unnoticed. The absence of the scenic designer was far more serious. It is rumoured that the management refused to pay his fare over.

'But that of course is part of the lunacy that attacks an enterprise which has so much money at stake. Suddenly there is a tightening of the purse strings just when it seems silliest.

'A serio-tragic incident of this type occurred towards the end of the run when Harry Secombe caught mumps. The other members of the company were summoned to the stage and told that the management would have those of the cast who had not had mumps inoculated against the disease. There was a large showing of hands and we never heard another word on the subject, possibly because injection would have cost around $20 a whack.

'Fortunately none of the company of *Pickwick* caught mumps, but they were all out of work during Thanksgiving Week and realized only too clearly whom they had to thank for that. An extra week could not have denuded the management to the bone.

'There are few things less attractive than the sound of a visiting actor criticizing the organization which has given him employment, and provided him with a living, which he may have taken from a native artist. But I cannot leave this country, which I admire and like so much, without a small word of exhortation. I have made a survey of the conditions under which the average actor lives and I am appalled by them.

'Rapidly the entire industry appears to be passing into the hands of producers, to whom the whole thing is a desperate fight for huge grosses. The personal touch or love of the theatre has almost completely disappeared and one can only exhort every one from the creative side to refuse to work unless they have contracts that will prevent them from being completely in the power of the operator.

'It is all wrong that every pre-Broadway show must be engulfed in the panic that seems to seize every producer at the absence of an Instant Rave notice from the first out-of-town critic they come up against. "What has gone wrong?" they hiss and scream at each other. "Someone must go," they continue. And out goes the director, the choreographer and the leading gent or lady but, never unfortunately, the producer himself. The latter, impelled by insecurity and lack of courage and imagination, is certain that the fault cannot be his, because has he not spent all that money on getting the show in front of an ungrateful public? But of course he has probably left out the most valuable factor of all, faith in what he must once have believed.

'This generalization does not only apply to musicals. In a recent production of Merrick's, the leading man (no, not the one who is reported to have given him a tiny biff in downtown Philadelphia recently*) was replaced. Now Merrick and the director were possibly perfectly right in this instance, but I only hope that the actual dismissal was dished out with courtesy and tact by one of them and not by a third person. It was a third person who informed the English artistes during the last week of *Pickwick* that the salaries and air tickets would be handed to us at the last performance.

'This was to ensure, I imagine, that we didn't do a midnight flit. I must point out that we were usually paid on

* Nicol Williamson when he was playing in *Inadmissible Evidence.*

Thursdays. It is this sort of thing that has made me feel I don't like being an actor much any more.

'I think conditions are slightly better in my native land, where the personal touch has not entirely vanished from the theatrical profession. But over here it does appear to me to be bogged down by bullying fear and possible humiliation and leaves the performer at the mercy of any unscrupulous or eccentric employer.

'There seems to be far more security and friendly atmosphere in a bank, a post office or even the subway, where there is, at any rate, a cop on hand to try and see that you don't get killed or even maimed in the jungle.'

This letter didn't really have much effect on anyone except actors who had suffered from Mr Merrick's whims and use of power. He replied facetiously to my allegations and I am bound to say that I found his response both puerile and humourless and quite unworthy of his undoubted talent at the invective.

Under the heading 'Merrick Answers Bull' he wrote:

'Thank you for permitting me to refute Peter Bull's personal version.

1. While true that *Pickwick* played to around $50,000 every week it was open, it sold discouragingly few tickets after the New York première. The average daily take was $900 and, had we run one more week, we would have grossed an appalling $25,000 for that week and less thereafter.

2. Naturally our ads. quoted holiday prices and schedules. We in the theatre for some strange reason live in hope.

3. The post-opening publicity was not negligible, despite the fact that for two weeks thereafter the newspaper strike persisted. Over $20,000 was spent on the purchase of TV and radio time and the show's principals appeared on most of the local and network radio and TV programmes, such as Ed Sullivan and Merv Griffin. Bull himself appeared twice on the Griffin show and my pub-

licity department offered him extraordinary aid in the American promotion of his book, including placing an article in the *New York Times* which appeared after *Pickwick* had already closed.

5. (For some unknown reason) The box office of the 46th Street Theater impressed me as one of the most cooperative, informative, truthful and polite groups of treasurers it has been my pleasure to work with.

6. Attempts were made to activate reduction in royalties, percentages and salaries, but to no avail. Three days after the New York opening, requests were made directly to London for reductions, but were rejected.

7. I did not speak to Harry Secombe because as a child I never had mumps, and I understand that it is quite serious in adult males, which might not be of concern to Bull.

8. Attempts were made all along the tryout route to insert revisions by a top playwright, Sindy Michaels (yes that was how he was misspelt in *Variety*) but cooperation from the Director and principals was negligible. New songs were even written by a talented young composer but the director and principals refused their cooperation in inserting these changes. Bull did not join the show until we had played San Francisco, Los Angeles and Cleveland.

9. Sean Kenny's work on the show was completed before the première at the 46th Street Theater and the sets functioned smoothly at the opening.

10. As regards the mumps inoculations, my physician advised me that there is no medical proof that the shots are in any way an effective deterrent.

11. Secombe's personal manager, Robert Kennedy, was advised well in advance of the closing of the strong possibility that we could not continue. The exact closing could not have come as a complete surprise to him.

12. I had no opening night party for *Luther*. When I do have opening night parties, every member of the company and crew is invited.

'By now this whole matter has become a total bore to me. As the producer, it was I who took all the risks. It was all the salaried and royaltied people who earned the money, and my decision to close when we did was not capricious but rather sound in the face of the public apathy toward the show.'

So wrote David Merrick. It was not worth pointing out that 'his' publicity department had nothing to do with my TV appearances or my articles in the *New York Times*. These were all set up by my personal friend, David Powers, who also happens to be the best press representative I have ever come across. He started working on my behalf during the *Luther* days and was not even remotely connected with *Pickwick*.

But I was delighted to get it all off my chest and in some way to fight back on behalf of dear Harry and the others. I was enormously flattered to find in Jack Gaver's book *Season In Season Out* a full account of the squabble. He summed up the whole affair admirably when he said, 'Whatever merit there may be on either side in the above, the exchange is a most enlightening one as to theatrical matters in general, as well as in this particular, and a vote of thanks is due to *Variety* for providing it with an outlet.' He also described it as 'one of the more diverting of several controversies destined fortunately to enliven a season that needed all of the extra-curricular help it could get, and was, unfortunately, missed by the general public'.

I haven't been approached by Mr Merrick to take part in any of his subsequent productions though, to do him justice, I do not think all the brouhaha would make the slightest difference to him if he really thought we could be of use to each other. And I feel exactly the same.

And now is the time to confess that I enjoyed every minute of the New York run of *Pickwick*, until the notice of closing was posted. It was an exceptionally easy evening for me, for which I was grossly overpaid. I loved the company and during the run I met the gent to whom I have dedicated this book. His name was and indeed is Don Lawrence. No it isn't. It's really Donald Lawrence Busby. The other is his stage name. During the tour and New York run of the show we hardly spoke, but he always intrigued me by his total detachment from the dramas that were going on. He just sat on the side of the stage reading some erudite work and when he did look up, there was always the suspicion of a cynical smile on his lips. Now most gentlemen of an ensemble are wildly gregarious but not this one. However, owing to the danger of possible malicious gossip, I thought it wiser not to make an approach during the run. But after the last matinée I could resist it no longer. I happened to find myself going out of the stage door at the same time as he.

'Look here, Don Lawrence,' I said, 'if I asked you out to lunch next week, would you scream the place down?'

'Certainly not,' he said briskly, 'my phone number is ...' and walked off down Forty-Sixth Street.

And so began a friendship which I have treasured beyond all the others I've had in my life and goodness knows I've had some wonderful relationships. Don shares my love of Greece and also the same birthday as Saint Spiridon, the patron saint of the Ionian Islands. His adjustment to the life out there has been remarkable and I would swear that he had been somewhere in the area in a previous existence.

He is sensitive, intelligent, unneurotic, cooks beautifully and is not remotely eaten up by ambition. He is an exceptional person and, as a matter of fact, I quite like him.

As a matter of further fact he has now seemingly settled down in London with his cat Theseus, and we have all three gone in to business together. The enterprise is an establishment called 'Zodiac', The Astrological Emporium.

By the way, thank you, Mr Merrick, for introducing me to my business partner!

8. *Doing very little in* Doctor Dolittle

In between appearing on Broadway in *Pickwick* and *Black Comedy* I was fortunate to get into a film which looked like being a gang-buster. At least that's what it was meant to be and it jolly nearly bust dear old Twentieth Century Fox. It was an attempt to repeat the fantastic success of *The Sound of Music* and was called *Doctor Dolittle*. It had the advantage of starring Rex Harrison, whose Professor Higgins had largely made *My Fair Lady* such a smash hit. The new film was based on Hugh Lofting's stories adapted and set to music by Leslie Bricusse, to whom I owed my involvement.

He had done the lyrics for *Pickwick* and when he and Anthony Newley were casting *The Roar of the Greasepaint* for America, they had offered the part of The Fat Man to me, heaven knows why. They were most persuasive but when they told me that a song or two might be required of me, I declined, though they said they could be *spoken*. Oh, how sick I am of this sort of thing! I mean people *speaking* songs, unless they are Rex Harrison who, I happen to know, studied how to do this for nearly a year. I did find out that Mr Robert Morley had been offered the role before me and between you and me and the gatepost I never imagine him as being the first choice for the part of I Pagliacci in the opera of that name. I know that he starred in the musical of *Fanny* at Drury Lane *and* played a season of cabaret at the Café de Paris, but then he has the Pluck of the Light Brigade and a great many guns, including an immensely lovable personality, wit and of course, beauty. Don't think I don't know which side my bread is buttered and I am hoping that his talented son Sheridan, whose godfather I am proud to be, will support me in my old age. His Noël Coward book has certainly made more money than those written by his father and me.

Talking of godfathers Sir Noël and I played the same roles at the christening of Sarah Jane McClelland, the daughter of Richard Leech, the actor, and his late deeply lamented wife, Helen. The part of the service had been reached at St Mary Abbott's in Kensington, where the priest asks the godparents if they'll renounce the Devil and *all* His Works on behalf of the infant. There was a slight pause and, in a panic, I said,

'We do,' at which the Master commented,

'Don't be so bossy, Peter.' Which nearly brought the church down.

All of which has nothing to do with *The Roar of the Greasepaint*, etc., but it has filled the best part of half a page and in these days of thin books and high prices, it isn't to be sneezed at. Anyhoo the noo, after I'd given Messrs Newley and Bricusse various reasons why I couldn't take part in their piece, I showed them the real reason. I dragged out of my wallet a dog-eared snap of my house in Greece. The job would mean neglecting it for a whole summer and I knew it would hate and resent me for that. I don't think you can go round building houses and then just leave them to get on with it. I find seemingly inanimate objects can be very human, like the chairs in my flat when I've neglected them for a long time. They look sulky until I have gone round and sat in all of them and then they lose that flat hard-done-by face.

Messrs Bricusse and Newley saw my point and were molto simpatico. In my opinion they were also extremely lucky as they got Cyril Ritchard to play the part, who was roughly a hundred and twenty-three times better than I would have been, though he had to be padded up to the nines.

Leslie obviously bore me no grudge, as when the question of *Doctor Dolittle* came up, he wanted to know if I was likely to be available and not tied up growing tomatoes in Greece. He would find it easier to write the part of General Bellowes, he said, if he was certain I would be playing it. The film was not starting till the late summer of 1966 and would mean my being able to spend several months in the Ionian before starting work. Enormously flattered I said,

'But, oh yes, I'd love to do it, Leslie,' and sat back and 'relaxed', whatever that greatly overworked word means. Half a mo! The Fowler Brothers say that it means 'to cause or allow to become loose or slack or limp', an explanation which certainly applied to me in those particular circs.

What I have never learned in my forty years with the entertainment industry (Is not that a wonderful title for a book? No, it is not!) is that the job is never yours until you actually start working on a set or a stage. And sometimes it can be whipped away from you even then, as happened to me at the Memorial Theatre in Stratford-on-Avon in the late forties. But that's another story and everyone is sick of it anyhow.

When negotiations first started for *Doctor Dolittle* I was in America recovering from my hassle with Mr David Merrick re *Pickwick*, and because I had been 'guesting' on a lot of TV shows, my American representative, Milton Goldman, thought I was pretty 'hot'. He was asking an astronomical sum for my services and appeared certain that we would get it. What I didn't realize (and possibly he didn't) was that the London office of my prospective employers, Twentieth Century Fox, were negotiating with my London agent at the same time and were discussing a much lower figure.

After a month or two of seemingly getting nowhere I was getting nervous and not without reason.

Suddenly Milton called me to say that a Mr Robert Morley, another artiste altogether, had been observed leaving Hollywood, where he had been appearing in a Kinematograph with Mr Jerry Lewis, carrying a script of *Doctor Dolittle* under his arm, when boarding a plane. As Mr Morley was also a client of Mr Goldman's the whole thing was a tidge embarrassing, and even I realized how much more valuable his name would be to the film than mine. It was Action Stations all right! I asked Milton to contact the London office immediately and try and clinch some sort of offer. I'd gathered a few days before that a contract was being mooted over there. Anyhow the ploy worked and a few hours later I seemed to have secured the job on *their* terms.

A few weeks afterwards I was having lunch with Mr Morley at Buck's Club, the British Institution started by his late father-in-law, Captain Buckmaster.

'And what are *you* going to do now, Bully dear?' asked Mr M. politely.

'A film with Rex Harrison,' I replied airily, 'called *Doctor Dolittle.*'

'Not, I imagine, the part of General Bellowes?'

'Yes, Robert, the part of General Bellowes.'

Mr Morley put his knife and fork down.

'Now you have gone too far,' he announced, 'you've actually begun to take the bread out of my mouth.'

He told me that on his arrival in London from Hollywood our agent(s) had informed him that the actor 20th Century Fox had thought was not available had suddenly become free.

'And,' continued Mr Morley, 'I hadn't even had time to read the script and turn it down.'

Practically always it's the other way round and he secures a role which I thought might come my way.

Anyhow in this case fate was kind and, after signing my contract, I took up residence in To Spiti Mou in Paxos until such time as I should be summoned to my employment. It was a happy feeling that I had 'my autumn fixed' as they say in theatrical circles, and that the only qualities seemingly required for the part of General Bellowes appeared to be a very red face, a loud voice and a certain talent for overacting. These, as any of you who saw *Tom Jones, Doctor Strangelove* or even *Alice's Adventures in Wonderland* will testify, are my three outstanding assets.

But it suddenly became obvious that I wasn't going to have everything my own way, and I hadn't even been in front of a camera yet. I received a telegram from my agent which said, '20th Century Fox requests you grow a beard and hair.' This threw me for a loop, as truth to tell, I have been trying to grow hair ever since I was in an epic called *Saraband for Dead Lovers* a couple of decades ago. They made me shave my head for that one in order that, as King George I of England, I could frighten the daylights out of my wife (the delectable Miss Joan Greenwood). They (the director and producer) assured me that my hair would grow ever so quickly and ever so much stronger after the shaving operation. This was not, I fear, strictly true and actually absolute rubbish. Since this capillary disaster I have been rubbing some liquid into my top-knot called Jochem's Hormone Tonic which some ass told me would turn me into a lady. It hasn't—so far. But it has stopped my remaining hairs falling out.

While I was figuring out what was the best thing to do, I got a registered letter from a Mr Eckhardt, who said, and I saw no reason to doubt him, that he was the production manager of *Doctor Dolittle*. It was a friendly letter, containing a most urgent request for my head measurements, in case I had to wear a wig. Apparently Mr Richard Fleischer, the director of the film, thought that I might not have time to grow my hair to the required period length, and goodness knows he was more than justified, albeit my Dundreary whiskers were coming on a treat. But although Mr Eckhardt had enclosed a super chart from the wig people, with coherent instructions about measuring a gent's cranium, both he and Mr Fleischer were unaware of two facts.

Living as I do on an extremely remote island, I had only a centrimetrical tape, and at the time of the arrival of the letter, I had no English speaking friends within sailing distance and my Greek had not yet even reached pidgin standard. Mr Eckhardt, however, wanted my head measurements by return, which meant getting them somehow on 'The Pullman', the ferry boat to Corfu, so called because of the arrangement of the seats. It was the only one of the three ferry-boats which could boast of an inside loo and it was due to sail at 10.30. Heaven knew when there'd be another chance owing to the etsi-ketsi state of the weather.

If only I could have waited till the following week when my friend Roger Furse (since sadly deceased) was due to arrive with his wife from the mother island. He could have whipped from 'temple to temple round back of head', as it said in the instructions, in a trice. He had an Oscar and designed most of Laurence Olivier's productions both for stage and film. And, as I'm an inveterate Oscar dropper, if Mr Eckhardt had wanted this sort of thing the previous year, that would have been all right too because Margaret Furse was over in Paxos and she's had two Oscars, one for *Becket* and one for *Anne of a Hundred Days* or thousand or whatever it was. These were awarded for her costumes and she is v. up in wigs as you can imagine. She was also the first Mrs Roger Furse, which is enough Furse dropping. Oh no it isn't. Because I've suddenly remembered two frightfully droll incidents connected with the distinguished couple. The first Mrs Furse who was born a Watts, married Stephen Watts, the writer, and they remained firm friends with her previous husband, Roger, and his second wife Inez, who had taken up residence in Corfu after his retirement.

They were all staying together when the mail arrived. Inez opened a letter addressed to her, read a few lines and handed it to Mrs Watts with the words,

'I think this is for you, Maggie darling.' And indeed it was for the first Mrs Furse, written by a lady who seemed not quite to be in touch, although the change-over had taken place some fifteen years previously. Another laughable incident was recorded in London, when the Wattses went to see the Furses off at London Air Terminal on their return to Corfu. Mrs Furse and Mrs Watts had gone on in front, and a fifth party with them asked where the ladies had got to.

'Those aren't ladies,' said Mr Furse, bettering the old music hall joke, 'those are my wives.'

Anyhow, to get back to my dilemma, re measuring my head, I decided that the only solution was to go and see Ho Raftis (Yorgos, the tailor of Lakka). He didn't speak a word of English but at any rate he must know about tapes, I mused. Armed with my Greek lexicon, and having written down the words 'nape' 'circumference' and 'forehead', I felt I might yet win through. It was already 9.30 so I had only about half an hour before the caique was likely to come into the harbour. At first sight there was no sign of Ho Raftis but I finally tracked him down at Mr Mouse's restaurant (the owner's name is Souris actually) where he was having a nice octopus breakfast washed down by a glass of retsina. Also present were or was about 20 per cent of the population of the village. I explained my problem as best as I could and Ho Raftis seemed cooperative and would I have some octopus? Impossible to explain that I'd just had a jolly good fry up in my own establishment up the hill. It simply isn't done to refuse any sort of hospitality in Greece, so I tucked in, though not with a vengeance, while he studied the wig chart. So did 20 per cent of the population.

I had to explain that it was for a film. The previous year I would have kept my great trap shut because, up till recently, I had been posing as an impoverished but decent and hard-working writer. This role suited me admirably as I was treated like an eccentric recluse. But since a Paxiot's aunt living in Detroit had caught me on one of the talk shows, I have had to abandon all pretence. In the old days I used to parry every enquiry with,

'Oh yes, I know the actor you mean. Everyone says he looks exactly like me.' They now know me in my true colours though they still cannot understand why none of my films ever reach the island.

Eventually Ho Raftis fetched his tape and I wrote the figures down and entered them on the chart. Suddenly I heard a toot from 'The Pullman' and rushed out of Mr Mouse's, still trying to masticate the rubbery octopus, and down to the jetty where I handed the envelope to Mitsos, the captain of the caique. It was only when I got back to To Spiti Mou that I realized that I'd forgotten to tell Mr Eckhardt that all the measurements were in centimetres and not inches. He would read that 'the circumference round the head back to front' was 61 and 20th Century Fux (as they once signed a telegram to me in Greece) would be convinced that they had engaged an artiste with two heads.

As a matter of fact they weren't best pleased with Ho Raftis's findings and I was ordered to report to London forthwith to have the job done properly. At first I demurred but my wise agent mentioned the possibility of another actor being engaged for my part and we'd had that one already had we not? So I hopped back to London, irritable but subsidized. I returned immediately to Paxos after my fitting and had a few slightly uneasy weeks, awaiting developments. The job was a valuable one as, owing to the stringent treasury rules at the time, every dollar counted, to put it mildly.

When I returned to England eventually the film company didn't seem all that keen on the immediate use of my services and I was on salary for at least six weeks before I was actually called. By this time the filming of *Doctor Dolittle* had become front page news. 20th Century Fox had taken over a beauty spot in Dorset called Castle Coombe and were bent on making the fullest use of the facilities it afforded. For starters they had dammed up a stream to make it represent a harbour. This caused a furore in the village but not as much as when they took down all the television aerials, as *Doctor Dolittle* was a period piece. Although the producers had supplied a master aerial, far better for viewing, the inhabitants grumbled vociferously, particularly those who were not actually making money out of the whole enterprise. Several rather ridiculous letters were written to the newspapers, questions asked in parliament, and everyone, in my opinion, seemed to lose their heads, especially a scion of the nobility who, with some other adventurous spirits, tried to blow up some of the film company's installations. Happily without success.

Even without all this tra-la-la, the film was running into very serious difficulties, as the weather was catastrophic. The unit was due back in Hollywood during August and they hardly managed to film more than a quarter of the scenes they had hoped to do in England. These latter included some of the scenes in which I (or General Bellowes) figured. However, in order to satisfy the Immigration Officials in America that I was essential to the film, I went down to Castle Coombe to make what is known as an 'Establishing Shot'. I stayed at Bristol during this period and motored over each day to the location. Here I met Mr Fleischer, the director, who has been responsible for a widely varied series of films from *Twenty Thousand Leagues Under the Sea* to *The Boston Strangler*.

I donned my gorgeous clothes for one impromptu shot. It's always exhilarating to wear clothes which haven't graced the bodies of Mr Morley or Mr Ustinov in other films, and Mr Ray Aghaian had designed for me a truly magnificent wardrobe including a series of spectacular hats. It was while wearing one of these that I ran into Rex Harrison, whom I had known slightly on and off through the years.

'You aren't going to wear that hat, are you?' he asked.

'I thought it was rather jolly,' I remarked.

He didn't refer to it again and was cordiality itself. And

that was that. At least, I thought it was, but as you will see later, it wasn't.

I walked down to a ravishing bridge by the stream and played a ridiculous short scene with the equally ravishing Samantha Eggar, whose uncle I was playing in the film. We made up our own words and had quite a giggle. Then I went back to London only to be informed that I would not be needed in Hollywood for several weeks. My lovely employers said they saw no reason why I shouldn't go back to Greece on full salary, which was remarkable of them, in view of the Great Wig Crisis. I took the precaution of asking that my American work permit should be sent to the Embassy in Athens, which I thought was a smart move at the time. I hadn't however reckoned on a strike by Olympic Airways to coincide with my leaving Greece. After a series of incredible but boring adventures, including sailing by night to Patras in what resembled a refugee ship, I reached Athens to find that it was a public holiday the next day and I had only twenty minutes to get to the American embassy but the officials were courteous and swift and I managed to get out of the city the next morning.

After a few days in London, I flew direct to Los Angeles over the Pole, a doubly exciting journey as I'd never gone that way and certainly not first class. On the way back I must confess that I flogged my ticket and the refund was enough to stand me a round trip to New York later in the year.

Still, first class or not, there was no one to meet me at the airport and I wandered round, feeling pretty like a very old Lost Boy. Eventually a message was passed through on the tannoy system that there was a car on the way for me. It took me straight to the Studios, which were hugely impressive. At that time Twentieth Century Fox were about the only firm to be making feature films. The *'Dolittle'* unit were out on location and no-one seemed to have the faintest idea as to when I might be expected to work. But I was given some invaluable pocket money and driven to a hotel on Hollywood Strip, where I had been booked in by my chum Hiram Sherman, who was doing a TV series with Tammy Grimes and was lodging just round the corner. My quarters were in a slightly seedy motel which suited me admirably with its nice swimming pool, large rooms, enormous fridge and slight air of wickedness, imparted by the odd call-girl or two and one call-boy on the premises.

Above all, though, it was noisy. It was right on the main highway which meant that it was fairly handy for a possible taxi. One of the gloomiest aspects of Hollywood for me is that I don't drive which makes living there alone torture for me, to say nothing of my friends who are unlucky enough to have to volunteer to transplant me from one place to another. My agent and I had entirely forgotten, in the excitement of the moment, to have any clause put in the contract to meet this state of emergency. I realized that most of my salary would go on hire cars as taxis were not all that reliable. So I was in deep trouble even before they started rolling the cameras on my fat face. However, by dint of a bit of blackmail ('Yes, I just made it this morning by changing buses at Beverly Hills but I don't know that I can guarantee to make it *every* day') I was able to cadge a lift conveying young William Dix, who was playing the very important part of the small boy in the film. He was out there with his Swedish mother and a tutor and proved splendidly untemperamental and totally unconscious of the extraordinary atmosphere which still permeates Hollywood.

The place certainly didn't seem to have changed all that much in the thirty odd years since I had last worked there. On that occasion I was to play a blacksmith in a film about and called *Marie Antoinette* starring Miss Norma Shearer and Mr Tyrone Power. It was nathless Mr Robert Morley, making his film debut as Louis the Something or other, who picked up the film and stole it without the slightest difficulty. I was cut out of the whole thing in an attempt to prevent this happening (our scenes were alone together), but perhaps it was all for the best as I was made to play the role with an American accent for some reason best known to the Messrs Metro, Goldwyn and Meyer.

Incidentally, on my return to Hollywood for *Doctor Dolittle,* I found that I owed the Screen Actors' Guild thousands of dollars in back dues, as I had omitted to get something called an Honorary Withdrawal Card when I had left in 1938. After much haggling and grizzling and whining from me, they did reduce my indebtedness but it was still quite a shock to my exchequer. This time I didn't forget, just in case I go there in 1998. Once every thirty years seems to be my quota.

I was to remain completely idle for the first two weeks but I did manage to get about a bit, thanks largely to dear Mr Sherman who ferried me to supermarkets, cinemas and friends, when he wasn't working.

Actually I got about quite a bit, though most of the time was spent by the swimming pool, watching the passing trade and pretty riveting *that* was. I also did a good bit of *dreading* my first day at the studio. I had already received a small fortune for nothing and that sort of generosity always makes me nervous. I somehow feel that they'll be doubly cross if I don't get it right! And of course my neurotic mind, aided by a few nightmares, saw no hope of winging my way through. Under ideal conditions it was conceivable.

But I had learned that I was starting off with my first big scene, which involved not only a very long speech to Rex Harrison but also a great deal to do with animals, and culminated in my leading a large plough horse out of Doctor Dolittle's surgery. So of course I was called to the studio on a Friday afternoon, which for actors is nadir time to start any kind of film, let alone one of epic pretensions, and with an epic budget. Everyone who's been working long hours all the week can't wait to get finished and away from it all for two days, and tempers have become frayed; consequently there is little tolerance for any terrified newcomer making a slip, or fourteen.

However, I put on my beautiful costume and *that* hat and was brought once again to be inspected by Mr Fleischer who said I looked lovely, so I perked up a bit. On the way back to my caravan (oh yes, it was one of those films. Rex had a whole house on the studio lot and very wise too!) I ran into Mr Harrison who said 'Hello' and gave the hat a sharpish look.

I waited about, with the butterflies by now whizzing back and forth in my stomach. I somehow knew in my heart of hearts that I was about to get my Comeuppance. And so it was. I was called eventually to the set and the first thing that unnerved me was that Mr Fleischer told me that he had thought about it a lot, and had decided that it would be better if I played the scene without my hat. Perhaps unfortunately I am not the sort of actor who can point out to the director on a first day in the studio that a character, coming straight from a fox hunt, would be unlikely to have his head nude, unless it has been explained in the text that the hat has been blown off in a sudden hurricane or whipped off by a whipper-in.

It was indeed a moment of truth. I had already taken a look at the set and that had reduced me to a state of terror. There were about thirty sheep there through whom I would have to force my way, and I didn't think (at first sight) that the horse who was playing my horse and I were likely to emulate Morecambe and Wise as a team. All the scenes I had in the film were with Rex and I suspected that his friendship and cooperation were likely to influence my being able to get through the film with at least a vestige of dignity to say nothing of morale.

I capitulated without a whimper and tossed The Hat to Mike Harte, my saintly Irish dresser. It was, I am convinced now, a wise move, for what followed that afternoon could have been even more catastrophic than it was had I not had the help and understanding of Rex.

The opening shot was one of Samantha and me bursting our way through a mountain of sheep and we managed that with a great many takes and not too many lines. But the next set-up nearly finished me. There was a long speech with a lot of place names and a great deal of movement, including the not absolutely easy one of leading a huge horse out of the set, wearing a huge pair of spectacles. Not me, the horse. Regarding the problem of lines there is a phrase which is used frequently by actors; 'I know them backwards.' This is a direct translation of what happened to me that particular afternoon. I not only knew them backwards but said them ditto. Subsequently I remembered the case of one of our most illustrious actors who had had a busy time with the prompter on the opening night of a pre-London tour. After a few lukewarm curtain calls, he turned to a fairly furious cast and said,

'Sorry chaps, I knew it at home,' which somehow made it all right as far as they were concerned.

I *always* know it at home and one of the reasons why I have never been able to enjoy acting is because I have an obsession, to a paranoic degree, about forgetting my lines. The first day on *Doctor Dolittle* was a definite example of learning the words *too* well. I went entirely to pieces on around the seventh take and finally the film actor's ultimate humiliation had to be used, viz. The Idiot Board, which is held on one side of the camera and contains the key words of the speech, in my case the lot, and magnified because of my eyesight.

Anyhow, after I'd got through it somehow in this haphazard and not very professional fashion, Rex came up and sympathized.

'I know what you're going through, old boy,' he said. 'It's those something animals. I couldn't get a line out at the beginning of the film because of the din they make.'

And perhaps it wasn't entirely my fault. Certainly there is nothing more disconcerting to an actor than hearing 'noises off' which haven't been rehearsed. That afternoon, besides the sheep and horse already listed, we had hens, owls, monkeys, parrots, dogs, birds and a few fox cubs. Rex was quite marvellous and I never saw him lose his temper with them once, maddening as they could be. It was usually a case of waiting for *them* to be ready and not some actor's wig.

As you can imagine, I spent a pretty fretful week-end, but, fortified by some 'anti-panic' pills, I managed to get through on the Monday without further disgracing myself. This reflects the maddening thing about filming. If, having once settled down and got to know everybody and everything on the set, one could go back and do the first scenes again, it would be far more satisfactory for all concerned, except perhaps the persons who have actually put up the money.

My most important scene in this movie was presiding as Magistrate at the trial of Doctor Dolittle at the end of which I had to sentence him to be detained in a lunatic asylum. It was a beautifully written and constructed episode and there was a fabulous dog to give evidence. He just barked the requisite number of times to inform the court whether he meant 'Yes', 'No' or even 'Maybe' and he did it impeccably. What the production staff didn't seem to realize was that animals are likely to get just as bored and tired doing the same thing over and over again as human artistes. Anyhow the dog got so exhausted some days that, by late afternoon, he was unable to get his dear front paws up on the dock as instructed.

The court sequence was to last quite a few days and at the end of it Rex had to sing one of the big numbers in the film, 'Why can't people be more like animals?'. The day before he was to embark on this, he treated us all to an extraordinary display of magic. After the 'wrap up', director Fleischer wanted to see a run through of how the song had been planned by Rex and Herbert Ross, the choreographer.

On an unlit and empty stage, with a musical play-back and in front of a handful of actors and technicians Rex showed us what he was going to do with the song. It was one of the most moving and exciting experiences I've ever known. After he'd finished there was a moment's silence and everyone burst into spontaneous applause, which is the sort of thing one hears about but so rarely happens. Yet, somehow, even though he did it perfectly in front of the camera, the atmosphere was never quite recaptured, but of course it had to be split into fragments for technical reasons.

I must confess that I quite enjoyed the Trial scene, once I had got through my long speech. I knew I hadn't been half bad and a reassurance from Rex put me in seventh heaven, as I regard him as the finest comedian of our time. But *Doctor Dolittle* was obviously running wildly over schedule and, though the money spent on it seemed inexhaustible, poor Arthur Jacobs, the producer, did suffer a minor heart attack in London. Luckily he has since recouped his losses and health on the *Planet of the Apes* series, where he learned that it was easier to cope with actors disguised as animals rather than vice versa.

Nerves were certainly getting a trifle frayed on the 20th Century lot around the early autumn of 1966 and I found that several scenes of mine were to be cut. However there was an essential one (I thought it so anyhow) still to be shot, but it was not scheduled till after the unit had returned from the Caribbean, where they were going to shoot all the island stuff, with which I was not concerned. The scene was an establishing one in which I arrived at Dr Dolittle's sister's house with a gouty leg, on which everything fell, like grandfather clocks, etc. You know the sort of thing. I was fitted for a plaster foot but that is as far as it went. They didn't renew my contract before the unit left Hollywood and I proceeded back to England. I did however intimate to my agents that I was perfectly happy to come back in December and complete my work in the film. They suggested a very reasonable figure as a retaining fee but 20th Century Fox were apparently not interested. I was consequently fairly astounded on viewing the finished film to see another gent, got up to look like me, receiving all the body blows in the scene, but his character was totally unexplained and made no sense at all.

However, I really didn't feel like complaining as I had had nearly three months in the Tinsel City and only worked about fifteen days during that time. Also I was getting handsome expenses as well as a salary, so I was able to stash quite a lot of moolah away against a sunny Greek day. I was being constantly entertained too by a series of remarkably enchanting people. The late Dame Gladys Cooper, inimitable and seemingly indestructible, waltzed me round the place from parties at the British Consulate to a hectic day at Disneyland. I had many happy quiet hours with Jean Simmons, marvelling at her everlasting youth and simplicity. Michael Wilding and Maggie Leighton, who suit each other so perfectly, were immensely kind and hospitable, and other Britishers, like James Fox and Stanley Holloway, flitted in and out of my life there.

I left Hollywood nevertheless without regret. The Strip on which I lived had got very violent and unpleasant, particularly at the week-end, and I had got rather sick of being entirely dependent on chums for enabling me to escape it. I flew back over the Pole contentedly clutching a fistful of dollars. And that was, I thought, the end of *Doctor Dolittle* and General Bellowes. But it wasn't.

Circa nine months later I was sitting on the terrace of To Spiti Mou minding my own business when the Post-Mule clocked in with a cable. Now it is absolutely certain that by the time one of these things reaches my residence, at least half the population will have been given a lively, if inaccurate, translation of the contents. This one was from my ex-employers, 20th Century Fox, and was two hundred words long. When deciphered it asked me if I would be willing to promote *Doctor Dolittle* in New York and elsewhere, and would I reply collect? All expenses were to be paid and the offer exactly suited my book, as I was just finishing one on Teddy Bears at the time and needed to hop across the Atlantic again to do a little more research.

But replying to the wire was another matter altogether. I was only just recovering from a state of shock induced by coping with a 'reply paid' one. Greeks are funny about this sort of thing. 'Twelve words reply paid' had been specified, and because I could not compress my message into under twenty, I gave the Post-Mule and its owner the extra money required. The Postmaster General of Paxos however would have none of it and sent them both back with instructions to me. Twelve words it had said and twelve words it was to be. I eventually solved the problem by running a lot of words together like 'SeeyounextSunday'. The P.M.G. appeared perfectly happy to accept this as a good old Anglo-Saxon word.

'Collect' was another thing altogether. It was a word apparently unheard of in the island; at least not in connection with cables. Eventually I had to pay for the reply myself. I also spent some extra money, pointing out to 20th Century Fix, as they now apparently signed themselves, that they owed me a hundred and ninety drachmas as a result of this. I did however mention that I accepted their proposal with delight. A cable came whirring back, expressing reciprocal pleasure but what the hell did all that stuff about drachmas mean? Would I reply collect please at once? Reply collect! I wouldn't, and indeed couldn't, so I sent an air letter to Hollywood pointing out that the company owed me a hundred and nine-five drachmas, including postage. And there the matter rested until I got back to London where, after some extremely grubby haggling, I settled with the London Office of the film company for two pounds and six shillings.

Just before leaving for New York the powers that be asked me if I would rather attend the opening of the film in Puerto Rico, which was simultaneous with the one on Broadway. I declined and they seemed astounded, but I expect they didn't know that I had never sampled the glamour of a full razzmatazz première, apart from seeing it in an actual movie, and I wasn't going to miss it now.

As things turned out, perhaps it would have been more cosy in Puerto Rico. It would certainly have been less strenuous. I can only tell you that I had hardly taken off my coat in my pad in Morningside Heights in very uptown New York, when the Publicity Department of 20th Century Fox were on the blower giving me a long list of the TV and radio shows in which I was expected to appear in the next three days.

I put my coat on again and whipped round in a semi-coma making a lot of unsuitable jokes about skunks. You see, I had been bitten *and* upstaged by a skunk during the making of the film and neither incident had happened to me before. Other points I brought out in publicizing the film were how all audiences, between the ages of nine and ninety, would love the film and what fun it had all been making it and how lovely everyone had been and how everyone had *adored* the animals, except possibly the skunk. It was all money (or expenses) for old rope as a matter of fact, but it did leave me a tidge exhausted for the actual première at Loew's State Theater.

This supposedly festive occasion had been organized like a vast military operation and I was strongly reminded of the Sicilian landings during the war. But in New York things were not to go so smoothly for me. We were all ordered to present ourselves (the principal artistes that is) at a chic bar near Central Park South and mass for zero hour. I had managed to secure my beautiful friend Ludi Claire, the writer and actress, as my escortee and we just had time to wolf down a quarter of a pound or so of best caviare, when we were summoned by a series of town criers to get into our limousine (Number 10 as it turned out). We glided luxuriously into Broadway and approached Loew's State Theater where arc lights and a great many persons crowded the sidewalks. I got terribly excited and clutched Milady, savouring my moment of triumph, after thirty-five years of slogging away at my art.

But, as we slowed down, people began peering in through the windows and hurriedly turned away. I heard a voice cry, 'Aw, it's *nobody*' in such disgusted tones that I sank back into the car, feeling rather like the late Marie Antoinette must have felt on the way to the guillotine. Shortly after this we came to a dead stop outside the main entrance to the cinema. I opened the door to descend only to get it slammed in my face with the words 'Not Yet! Not Yet!' by an officious official. I cowered in my corner until we were ordered to emerge. I was then roughly parted from Miss Clare and hustled up to a small platform, where a handsome and totally composed television interviewer was conducting proceedings in front of a barrage of cameras.

'Here's Peter Bull, one of the many stars of the film,' he announced kindly, 'with the Californian tan still on his face.' As it was well over a year since I'd finished my role in the film I found myself saying it all came from a sun lamp in downtown Chelsea, London, which didn't help any of us very much, and, after a series of similar inanities, strong hands whipped me off the dais and I was allowed to rejoin lovely Ludi.

From then on we were on our own, which should have been all right but wasn't. We were passed through a roped off section and on our way to the auditorium, when I realized that this was probably the last time I could go to the 'loo' with impunity. I jumped over the barrier, only to be sharply rebuked by an attendant.

'You can't go there,' he barked.

'I want to go to the Rest Room,' I explained.

He ignored this.

'But I'm in the film,' I whined. 'I'm one of the stars.' Neither of these statements made the slightest impression on him and he continued to bar my passage. Finally I gave it up and beat a humiliating retreat down the richly upholstered carpet, taking a furtive glance behind me to see if

I was going to be hounded out of *my* film première. I was a desperate man however, and, seeing a gap in the barricades, I crawled on my hands and knees under the rope in my dinner jacket and eventually achieved my end.

On my return from the bowels of the building, we entered the auditorium which was almost entirely empty and deeply depressing. It took about half an hour for the theatre to fill up (most of the customers had paid £50 per seat for A Charity and for that price had a right to be Heard and certainly SEEN). Eventually the lights began to dim, the curtains parted and the actual film started. The opening titles were greeted with thunderous applause and then the actors' names were flashed across the screen to wild acclaim —Rex Harrison, Samantha Eggar, Anthony Newley and Richard Attenborough were equally well received. Then the curtains for some unaccountable reason closed slowly, completely blotting out *my* name which happened to be the next credit title. However I suppose that even this sort of treatment is still preferable to being called Peter Bell or Ball, as frequently happens, to say nothing of Peter Dull, which was the name I appeared to act under, when appearing with Mr Albert Funney in the Paris run of *Luther*.

Anyhow at Loew's State Theater I slunk or slank back in my seat prepared for anything. My companion says that I had a series of zizzes and she had to hit me during my scenes. In which case I had plenty of sleep that night. By this time I didn't mind if I had, as so often, ended up on the cutting room floor. But not a bit of it! There I was, thirty-eight times larger than life, leering out from the screen in Glorious Panavision, Cinemascope and Something Colour, which made me look like an apoplectic baboon.

Curiously enough I rather enjoyed being in *Doctor Dolittle* at the cinema because for once I had no angst about remembering my lines. And although it received harsh treatment from press and public alike at the time, I have no doubt but that the film will eventually get back all the money spent on it, both at Christmas time showings for the kiddiwinks and eventually as a big television attraction. I'm sure I hope so because for films made in Hollywood actors get residuals.

IV

LIFE IS A CUCUMBER IN TEDDY BEAR LAND

9. *Bear with Me*

NOW that the Teddy Bear book has been launched on both sides of the Atlantic it is interesting (to me at any rate) to note the effect the little furry creatures have had on my ordinary way of life. It all seems to have been going on for years. As a matter of fact it has.

For those of you who haven't read *Bear with Me* (and judging by the royalties returns your name is Legion), I got involved in the subject about seven years ago, after realizing what a surprising influence the Teddy Bear has had on mankind since the beginning of the century. This conclusion was reached during an evening in New York, when I found that three out of five people at dinner had had traumatic experiences with or because of their Teddies. I was one of the three. Mine was when I returned from school and found that the mater had given away my beloved friend to a jumble sale. I couldn't show my full anguish as I did happen to be sixteen at the time. And in those days for schoolboys virility was 'in'. Little did I know that one day my current bear 'Theodore' would receive an invitation to lunch from Archibald Ormsby-Gore, who belongs to the Poet Laureate himself. But that's skipping things a bit.

I decided to write a symposium about the animals and set

about my task with relish, enthusiasm and a seriousness which frightened the daylights out of my close friends. But the research proved a far more complicated affair than I had envisaged. It involved correspondence of alarming proportions, visits to arctophilists in Britain and America, and the studying of old papers, books and magazines.

But it was all immensely worthwhile and, during my peregrinations, I got to know some astonishing people, and letters are still pouring in from all over the world. Today, I must say, was quite exceptional. There was a missive from a lady in Bradford who wanted a small teddy like Theodore and could I send her one C.O.D. I didn't like to tell her that I was running an Astrological Emporium and not a toy one. There was a letter from the Teddy Bear Museum in Virginia, which is a sort of home for retired Teddy Bears. Mrs Iris Carter, who runs it, collects documents, old children's books and anything remotely connected with Teddy Bears. Then there was a newspaper clipping from the *States Item*, published in New Orleans, showing the children of the A. D. Crossman Elementary School celebrating Theodore Roosevelt's birthday. It was the President who started the whole dotty but lovely mystique. Anyhow the kids wrote to me and posed with their Teddies round a copy of the American edition of my book.

But undoubtedly my most important contact has been Colonel Henderson, a retired Scots officer, who has a small army of bears (around the two hundred mark actually) of every type and material. He is a man of great personal charm and treats the whole thing even more seriously than I do.

'Let's have a rally for the little chaps,' he once said to me, adding, 'I don't think the Albert Hall would be too big, do you?' I agreed with him, knowing full well what had happened at a small village in Norfolk, called Brundall, which had held its Annual Fête. This time, in the list of attractions, a Teddy Bear competition was announced, with prizes for the oldest, the most beautiful and the best dressed

Teddy present. Just 1,500 entered for the occasion. So I am thinking that the Albert H., renovated though it will be and a trifle forbidding for this sort of thing, may very easily not be big enough for the Great Teddy Bear Rally. Perhaps we could take the whole thing outside to the Park and have a real T.B.'s Picnic.

On the day the British version of my book was published, I gave a small ... No that's wrong! Theodore, my bear, gave a small tea party in the Roosevelt Room at Brown's Hotel. He had decided that it had just that old-fashioned but richly upholstered veneer to provide him and his friends with a perfect setting. The latter were an interesting lot and provided the staff of the hotel with food for thought.

There was, for instance, 'Buzzy' from Colchester, who was made Archdeacon of the Marshes and is now well into his sixties. He was in the Church for a long period but was perfunctorilly defrocked for going over to Rome, after he had been left with some Catholic friends during the school holidays. He then went into the Merchant Navy but flat feet and an excess of rum played havoc with his nautical career and he now lives a semi-retired life with his lifelong companion, Miss Winifred Seaton. He is reported to be writing his autobiography.

Some of the guests came from even further afield. Edward from Somerset had recently had some new growler chords fitted, as his own had been trodden on when he was a cub, and only recently has medical science supplied the answer. He growled at me with pleasure (through his interpreter) and I growled back.

Sir Gangy de Brownman Bt. arrived from the Isle of Wight. He is a very classy naval type bear and a close friend of Sir Alec Rose's Algy, the distinguished rabbit, who accompanied the sailor on his historic voyage. He is the first Bear Baronet (that I know of) and was decorated for services in the field. When asked point-black by Theodore 'What field?' Sir Gangy replied 'Ploughed, silly!'

He always corresponded with Theodore so I never found

out with whom he lived. I just knew that the address was that of a rather grand sounding house near Ryde. When I was asked to appear on the TV programme 'Magpie', the producers asked me to bring some other bears. So I wrote to Sir Gangy who said he'd be delighted and what was the Rig of the Day?

I told him to dress as smartly as possible and was not remotely surprised to find him turn up in his Admiral's regalia, complete with black tie and medals. He was accompanied by a very nice couple who said they were looking after Sir Gangy while their son, a Naval Officer and his owner, was at sea. Knowing that we were in for a long tiring day at the studio before transmission, I asked them if they'd like to see the show on my TV set and then I would return Theodore's co-star to them, as they intended to return to the Isle of Wight that night.

Sir Gangy and I followed Theodore and his lot into a car and we were transported to Teddington Studios. The 'Magpie' people couldn't have been more friendly and Tony Bastable, who was to interview us all, had brought his friend, a battered veteran of two wars, one Baron Wolfgang de Berrenhausen, apparently a survivor from Baron Von Richthoven's Flying Circus, but who had defected to us after World War I. Sir Gangy and he got on like two bear gardens on fire and Theodore, I am ashamed to say, sulked a bit, particularly when he noticed with his eagle eye how many close-ups the baronet was given during the actual transmission. After all, even Teddy Bears are human.

When we had finished, we were driven back to my flat where Sir Gangy's male escort was waiting for him. His good lady had already departed, but both had been delighted by their protégé's performance on the small screen. I was about to introduce David Macfarland, one of the producers, when I suddenly realized that I didn't know the surname of Sir Gangy's friends.

'Clark,' said the gentleman quietly.

'And this is Mr Clark,' I told David.

'Admiral Clark, as a matter of fact,' said the gentleman even more quietly.

All these *petites histoires* (I can't be belle lettering all the time) are to try and demonstrate to the cynics and unbelievers that we arctophilists aren't all half-way round the bend or moronic never-grown-up psychopaths. It was astonishing to see how the Press responded to us all on that sunny October afternoon in Brown's Hotel. As it was Theodore's party, he'd insisted that it should be a proper picnic and no drinks would be served. So it was tea, hunney, ice cream and balloons. At one moment I was asked by the photographers to take most of the bear guests into Berkeley Square, which I did happily. What made the whole expedition so enjoyable was that I was followed by a cavalcade of the owners, who were not so much nervous of their charges being stolen by an unscrupulous person as anxious to make sure that the best profile was being chosen and that all the costumes had been properly adjusted.

None of the people in the street paid the slightest attention but the resultant publicity was staggering. We had most of the back of *The Sun* for starters. But like all Minority Groups we have our detractors and some of the reviewers of the book declared it a tidge too saccharine for their taste. I can't say I blame them. I feel exactly the same about books on horses, lions, cats or, I imagine, what They call Real Bears.

The book in Britain certainly didn't get in the charts and indeed I occasionally get irate letters from dear Messrs Hutchinson about the money I owe *them*, but the number of people who seemed to get hold of copies was considerable and quite a percentage of them took the trouble to tell me how relieved they were to find how many distinguished people still had great affection for their Teddies. Up till now they had thought it faintly indecent to go banging on about their treasured animal, but they were entranced to find themselves in the company of Dame Margot Fonteyn, Dusty

Springfield, Lynn Redgrave, Sir John Betjeman, Richard Hearne, and the late Sir Donald Campbell, to name but a few.

10. *The Teddy Bear Book*

THIS was the title of the tome in the United States and a jolly good one it was too. Unfortunately it was not possible to call it this in England as Margaret Hutchings had used it for a book on the same subject which was largely devoted to the making of the Teddy Bear. Delightful as it was, it didn't really cross my territory at all but it had been published in 1964, which was only a few years before I had hit on the idea for my book.

The American venture started in the most bizarre way possible. Bill Holden, now the owner of the Strathmore Book Shop in Regents Park, but then a director and head of publicity at Heinemann's, had given me introductions to several of his opposite numbers in New York, as I was hoping to flog some of my published works the other side of the Atlantic. Among his friends was a gentle lady called Jean Ennis, who was enchanting to me and we got on tremendously well together. I confided in her a lot and one day she asked me to have lunch with her and a friend.

Half-way through the meal, she said to me, 'Tell Jim about your Teddy Bear book.' I had already banged on a good deal to her about it at a previous meeting, but I promise, with no ulterior motive. So I started on my party piece and when I'd finished, her guest said 'I'll buy it', and handed me his card which said 'James Silberman, Vice-President of Random House'. I must point out that at this moment I had made no plans for a British production, let alone American. Also, I hadn't written one chapter.

Contrarywise, I was currently appearing in the American production of Peter Shaffer's excruciatingly funny play *Black Comedy* at the Ethel Barrymore Theater in New York. I played the part of the Colonel, who keeps on falling out of a rocking-chair. It was an easy evening for me, as the comedy formed the second part of a double bill and I didn't have to get to the theatre until nine o'clock.

Other advantages of the engagement were that we were under the management of Mr Alexander Cohen, who actually likes actors. This made a change from Mr David Merrick, who doesn't. Also the delectable Lynn Redgrave played my daughter and we hit it off from the first rehearsal onwards. It's the only play in which I've appeared, whose first night was postponed by a blizzard. I've always dreamed of this sort of thing happening and went skipping up and down Broadway in the snow in high glee. Finally we opened on a Sunday.

Random House offered the (to me) staggering sum of £2,000 as an advance and I spent some of that cabling my agent in England, Joyce Weiner, to accept it without reservation. But, as things turned out, I was a trifle hasty in my excitement. It was 5 April 1967 that all this happened and it was assumed by me that we could expect publication by the beginning of 1968. Silly old me!

However I was able to continue with my research on Teddies and, as my part in *Black Comedy* wasn't too strenuous, I could bounce around Manhattan like a Sorbo and deal with the voluminous correspondence which came in as a result of some TV appearances. When the time came to up sticks, leave the play and push off to Greece I took all the gathered material with me and tried to piece it together.

Now the trouble with all us Aries people is that we take

up new enterprises with enormous enthusiasm and, quite often, astuteness, but we tend to lose interest very quickly, particularly if one is as lazy as this particular Arian. I have so often gone into the problem of the Loneliness of the Short Distance Writer and in my case it is practically pathological. I'll do anything to get out of putting fingers directly to typewriter for creative purposes. Particularly on Wednesdays. Why Wednesdays you may well ask? Well ask away!

Wednesday in England is the last day on which I dare send away my pools and the solutions to the competitions which have littered my desk since Sunday. Anyone would think I was planning a vast invasion of some foreign country, involving the use of elephants, judging by the mess. Piles of newspaper clippings, stamps, envelopes and tranquillizers are all mixed up together and heaven help anyone who disturbs or disarranges them.

It all started in 1952 when I won eighty-three pounds six shillings and eightpence in 'The Most Popular Blouse' competition from the *Sunday Empire News* and, if only I hadn't, life would have been very much easier ever since. Not that I was alone in this particular achievement. I shared the 750 pounds prize money with eight other lucky readers, including a Mrs Dick.

Since this seemingly fortuitous occurrence it has been extremely difficult to get on with any career, theatrical or literary and/or enter into matrimony or any other semi-permanent arrangement. The fact is that I cannot resist entering every competition I can lay my peepers on. Long ago I spent the last of the eighty-three pounds six shillings and eightpence on stamps and postal orders.

In the meantime, just in case I don't win any more, I'd better get a move on with the Great Teddy Bear Saga as it's now Thursday and I have no excuse for not so doing. A more unsuitable place than Greece to assemble data I cannot think of. To begin with there is always a bit of wind in the afternoon, and I promise you it's not one of those ghastly *double entendres*, but the papers go whirring round the garden and get covered in salt from the sea and it's all hell. In those days, I thought the letters which I'd received from the Teddy Bear lovers of the world were so fascinating that they really only needed reproducing in their entirety for the world to realize that the mantle of Lord Chesterfield letter-writingwise. (What a dreadful word!) had descended on my shoulders.

So I gathered them all together in their appropriate sections and they did form at least two-thirds of the MS. And on my next visit to New York I presented them cheerfully to Mr Silberman, expecting to be summoned to a banquet in the Algonquin and told that I was in the running for the Nobel Prize at least. Not a bit of it. He just threw it all back at me and said it wouldn't do at all. And he was perfectly right. It was, I suspect, sheer laziness which had driven me to such foolishness in the first place. Anyhow with my tail slightly between my legs I slunk away to my pad and started rewriting or rather co-ordinating the letters into a less indigestible form.

I managed to churn out a specimen chapter while still in New York, which apparently passed muster with both Mr Silberman and the gentle editor he had assigned to me, one Miss Margaret Harrell who was a real charmer and gave me some spiffing lunches on Random House. It was obvious that there wasn't the slightest chance of the tome coming out in 1968 and that I would have to devote another summer to its completion in Greece. Again the agony of sheets blowing into the Ionian, losing treasured snaps of old Teddies and forcing myself to revise and revise. However I was able to clock the finished article in on 25 September 1968, it being Margaret Harrell's birthday.

After that there was a lull, until I heard from Mr Silberman that (a) he liked the book and (b) that Miss Harrell was ill and I had a new editor. He also intimated that it was essential that I go over to discuss the illustrations for the book. So I popped over for Christmas. Anyhow I was by then far more used to spending it in New York, and just as well, for every year at this time I find a sadness coming over me, since the death of my mother.

A remarkable lady in every way, she used to make the festive season so delightfully unfestive and undemanding. What she liked best was the family coming to tea and *that* didn't interfere with her faithful maid's plans. Jessie liked to go to Harlesden on that day, so it meant having Christmas lunch round about twelve, which wouldn't have suited us at all.

It all became a ritual for me. I used to go to Chelsea Old Church for Communion and then slip into my mother's for a cup of coffee. My duties were simple. Just to arrange the Christmas cards. She (or Jessie) hated having them up before ('they just collect the dust, dear'), and there was certainly no nonsense about keeping them up till Twelfth Night. There was also no question of a Christmas Tree, except for the silver one which had belonged to my grandmother and whose leaves were getting more and more fragile every year. But part of the Christmas Tree programme was for every member of the family to choose a candle on the tree and put a sixpence in the kitty and the owner of the longest surviving one would scoop the pool. It usually ended in the mater having to fork out most of the money and, I fear, rarely winning the contest.

All the male members of the Christmas Tree Party found on their plates a pair of socks (always of sober hue) with a generous cheque inside. I remember once a favourite niece bringing the gent to whom she was engaged at the time who, not unnaturally, did not have a cheque in his socks. Actually my mother wasn't all that keen on him, and when the match was broken off she did ask me if I thought that the young gentleman would return the socks. I never knew if she was being serious. I had heard of rings, etc., being returned in the heat of the moment but never step-grandmother's socks.

The afternoon used to end with a heady game of 'Happy Families', accompanied by a good deal of unpleasantness because of the Bull conventions which I have never heard of being played by anybody else. The point was that if one was lucky enough to find Miss Chop the Butcher's Daughter At Home, one had to say 'Thank you' in a loud clear voice. Should one forget this little display of good manners, any other player could shout 'Pepper' and take the card away. The interesting thing is that I still have the same cards and, whenever my two brothers come to dinner, we play the game and, I'm afraid, still have the same sulks and quick outbursts of temper. 'But I *did* say "thank you"', we scream at each other.

Anyhow this is a sufficient digression from the Teddy Bears and it really has nothing to do with the little dears or has it? In fact there I was in New York for the third or fourth Christmas in succession with a plastic tree which stands permanently in the dark dining-room and makes it festive all the years round and gets dusted at least once every two.

The winter of 1968 seemed a most promising one. My new editor at Random House was a brilliant young chap called Steven Aronson who seemed to know roughly what I was talking about and everyone cheerfully predicted that the book would come out with a great flourish in the autumn of 1969. As I had just flogged the bloody thing in England it is interesting to note that Random House said rather grandly that the British publishers could copy the American edition and indeed photograph it, to save expense.

I only announce this fact because, by a merry quirk of fate, the book was sold to Hutchinson's a year and a half after the Americans bought it and, in fact, came out exactly a year earlier.

At first everything seemed to go well. With publication assured both sides of the Atlantic I went back to England merry as a grig. Steven Aronson wrote me long funny letters and urgent photographs and proof corrections went whirring back and forth. In order to be ready for the American bookstores by Christmas 1969, the tome had to go into production by 1 March. 'I am sharpening some pencils and stocking up on black Japanese magic markers which cut through paper like blow torches in this chill latitude,' wrote Mr A. He admitted he had cut a lot of the more saccharine stuff but cheered me by saying that he thought the book was 'very amusing' and 'could bc dynamite on the market'. I did however insist on the excision of phrases like 'Gotten' which he tended to insert from time to time.

It was around March of 1969 that I suspected things weren't going all that well. Long long silences, followed by long long telegrams, and I thought it was probably worthwhile investing in a further trip to America, on one of my charter flights. And it is here that I must confess that I've travelled across the Atlantic in a variety of guises from being an American Friend of English Soccer (with rattle) to a member of the Edgeworth Athletic Club from the Bronx. I was once a North American Student and I am here to tell you I wasn't anywhere near the oldest student to totter off the plane, although I was almost suffocated by the fumes that had emanated from the cigarettes of the younger members during the flight.

It has always seemed to me idiotic to pay the full fare in any aircraft if one can go for less than half-price and have the extra money when one gets there. I am a member of at least six organizations who have affiliations with other societies and, though the Board of Trade tried to pin me down once on the illegality of one of my flights, I think I had a cast-iron case. Granted that flights are delayed, that one has to go from the not always convenient Gatwick, it's still nicer to make two trips for the price of one.

So I hootled across in the spring of 1969 and it was just as well I did. Mr Aronson was moving away from the city to work elsewhere. But he'd done a masterly job on cutting and readying the book and I shall always be grateful to him for his hand in the eventual product. I was then presented with my third editor (Goodness! I seemed to have a lethal effect on them) one Sally Kovalchick, a wonderful friend and, in my opinion, vastly under-rated by her employers.

She was a great chum of Steven's and, until he left, they worked together.

But the publishing heads still hadn't decided on a format or a cover. There was one desperate moment when somebody in the Art Dept suggested that it would be a good idea to have it in black and white, quite simple like *Portnoy's Complaint*, they said. I did point out that the two books didn't have much in common and finally we decided on a delightful montage from old postcards of the period and it must be admitted that the final cover was impeccable apart from a picture of me on the back, looking more sinister than usual, as a large portion of my head seemed to have been chopped off.

Anyhow we had a busy time choosing all the photographs and an even busier time trying to get 'Permissions' about which they are frenetic in the States. They don't seem to care a hoot about libel but just the mentioning of somebody's name, usually in a more than favourable way, necessitates endless correspondence. However I left Sally to deal with that and pressed on home to England, where the proposed British edition was progressing at high speed, possibly too high.

I was soon off to Greece again, thinking how exciting it was going to be with two versions of my book appearing almost simultaneously both sides of the Atlantic. We had however arranged a gap of a month so that we could manage the publicity side of it better. But in the middle of July I got two letters from Random House which shattered my dream.

The first I opened was a shock. It came to Paxos direct and was from Sally telling me that the whole format of the book was to be on a larger scale and that instead of it costing $5.95 it was going to be around the $10 mark. But, for some reason, which I haven't fathomed, it meant that it would not be published until the spring of 1970.

The second letter was from Jim Silberman via my literary agent in which he said he didn't anticipate publication till the autumn of 1970, which indeed turned out to be accurate. It meant that I would have to wait that much longer (a year) for any royalties but what really annoyed me was the waste of time, effort and, above all money, which had been so lavishly spent during my frenetic visits to New York and back. However I replied civilly and nobly.

On 1 August Mr Silberman wrote and said how relieved and grateful he was to receive my calm letter and Sally wrote a few days later, assuring me that she wouldn't desert me in my hour of need and there was no question of a fourth editor being required.

Where I was mad, in the light of subsequent events, was to agree to a reduced royalty owing to a sudden bonhomie and genuine regret at the postponement which came wafting across the Atlantic. It had been pointed out to me that because of the increased cost of the book we should all make sacrifices. That meant me *all*. And although you may be getting bored with this welter of seeming trivia, it is just possible it may be useful info. for any author who is thinking of having a book published in America.

There is a subtle difference between the organizations of the two countries, the British never say that they are efficient and indeed aren't. The Americans say they are and it's simply not true. At least neither in the theatre or publishing world. They all *mean* to be but they are always let down by the X factor, whether it is the stage hands who, on the second night of *Luther* in New York, couldn't be found to lower the curtain or the Sales Dept of Random House who ran out of copies of *The Teddy Bear Book* three weeks before Christmas, a tome they'd cheerfully advertised for many months as being the Ideal Gift.

But I'm anticipating things and we are nowhere near publication date yet, let alone actually selling the damned thing across the counter. After we'd all got over the initial frustration of the postponement, there was a lull till October when Sally came over to England herself and I agreed to return her visit in the winter of 1969, as by this time additional problems had presented themselves. The publicity gent for Steiff's the German toy manufacturers who are the most favoured contestants for the title of the original Teddy Bear Makers but not, in my opinion, the winners, was cutting up rough about giving us any photographs of the very old bears, which Miss Marguerite Steiff, from a wheel chair, had constructed. She had polio but spent her life making the finest soft toys in the world. They are still doing so and it's ten to one that the most attractive bears you see in the shops these days come from Geinigen, where the factory is.

A further complication was that *Time* magazine did a fine little piece on the British version of the book and Americans enquired after it in the bookshops and were confused by the fact that it was called *Bear With Me*, whereas its autumn publication had been announced by Random House under the title of *The Teddy Bear Book*. And it was only possible to obtain the British version in New York at the British Book Center.

I flew out just in time for Christmas, ironed a few things out and we all really seemed to be getting a move on. Jean Ennis arranged lunch with a young lady from *Life* magazine, who, it would seem, would want to do an entire feature on the book. A year later it did indeed do four pages or so on The Teddy Bear with pictures of all the people I supplied the names of, leaving me out entirely and mentioning the book once briefly. Better than nothing, I do see, but disheartening and it was only, by a continuous barrage from my friends to the 'Letters' section that they finally published a minute picture of me sitting in Berkeley Square with the bears. It was particularly galling as I had flown back to New York during the promotion tour and had had hundreds of snaps taken by an eccentric foreign lady, who was *Life*'s own photographer. They were sensationally good, which made the whole affair even more mysterious, including a photo of Theodore sitting on my hand, which was quite beautiful.

11. *I'm a Nut Case*

FROM the semi-fantasy world of the Teddy Bear to the completely ditto of the film commercial.

During this visit to New York I got a startling offer to go to Barbados to play the part of the Commodore in a 'Fish Fingers' commercial, which I accepted with alacrity, even though it was to be a 'visual', which in those days was still deemed to be a bit common. Nowadays, when even Lord Olivier is behind a Polaroid camera, it is the height of chic. And of course a commercial location can be an enormously attractive stint. I would have thought, under the circumstances, that it would have been simpler to go straight to the West Indies from New York. But no, I had to go back to London to sign the contract. However the more one gets mixed up with the Advertising World, the more one realizes that time, not money, is everything. The finished product of one of these films rarely lasts more than a minute on the TV screen and it's breathtaking to think of the cost of such an undertaking and the risk of money going down the drain, if the client doesn't like the results.

On the other hand the risk is minimized by employing the finest directors and cameramen in the business, and the layman would be astonished if I reeled off a list of names who have contributed to TV commercials, both actors and technicians, in the last decade. The actor therefore has every chance of not looking a fool and an unprofessional one at that. I found that being 'Commodore Bird's Eye' did me quite a power of commercial good.

The fares of the unit and myself to Barbados on this occasion must have amounted to well over £3000. The supporting cast was composed of local small boys, British Residents and v. keen on the product we were all pushing, 'Fish Fingers'.

The plot of the film was comparatively simple. Commodore Bird's Eye was signalling from shore to Captain Bird's Eye (afloat but luckily unseen or the residuals would have been smaller for me!) that there were a new type of Fish Finger on the market, crisper, tastier and more luscious than experienced before. Later on my crew (none of them over ten years of age) and I were seen at sea eating the product. The fact that we had to eat them in the boiling sun at a temperature of about 110 degrees didn't seem to affect the boys' enjoyment in the least but it did cause the lady who was frying them in (and I quote) 'new, even more crispy toasted breadcrumbs' to throw up several times. She had to work on one tiny jet on a small grill in a midget galley aboard a phoney pirate ship called, surprise surprise, *The Jolly Roger*.

It was, it must be admitted, a very strenuous time and not at all the lovely languorous West Indian holiday one assumes from the travel posters. It was also very much a Do It Yourself enterprise. There was never a question of a make-up gent or a wardrobe mistress (or master) and I had to cart my period wig, sword, hat and most of my costume, not only from London, but the length and breadth of most of the beaches in Barbados. Some of the shooting took place near the Hilton Hotel and the American customers seemed riveted by our carryings-on, perhaps thinking it was all part of some old native ritual and that the Fish Fingers were the bones of our fish ancestors.

On the other hand it needs something pretty sensational in the film-making line to be taking place in the King's Road nowadays, where they are so accustomed to scenes being shot that even Mick Jagger didn't collect much of a crowd when he was acting there in broad daylight.

I remember years ago when Alec Guinness was making *The Horse's Mouth* there. A scene was being shot outside Tucson's, the jeweller and pawnbroker, and Alec was using my flat, a hundred yards away, as a sort of dressing-room cum resting-house. He is the most modest and unassuming of actors but even he was surprised at the lack of interest maintained by the good people of Chelsea as he wheeled a large upright piano into the shop.

'But, Alec,' I explained, 'people are always doing that sort of thing in the King's Road on a Saturday morning. You can't expect them to stop their shopping every time it happens.'

Out in the West Indies however we were obviously a considerable Tourist Attraction. We had a frightfully efficient and talented director, Cliff Owen, and the unit worked like blacks, if you will forgive the expression. And a lot of you won't I do see. But you know what I mean. When I returned to London, Mr Owen and the unit were to press on to Jamaica to toss off another commercial or three, in which I was unfortunately not involved.

I did however get mixed up with an operation for a grumbling appendix. And it wasn't the only thing that grumbled. I knew I would have to do some post-synchronization on the commercial, owing to the noise of the sea, throwing up, tourists, etc., and I'd warned the Advertising Agency of my approaching non-availability. Unfortunately they couldn't cut the film before I was cut in the hospital and one opportunity was missed.

I was detained longer than I'd meant or indeed *was* meant to be, and suddenly 'The Client' wanted to see the finished 'Fish Finger Film'. What to do? I suggested to Barry Myers, the advertising producer, a courteous, unbrash gentleman, that there were two alternatives as I thought I was really too ill to carry out my duties satisfactorily. One was to secure the services of my friend John Moffatt, who does a very passable but highly libellous imitation of me, or those of Mr Robert Morley, who doesn't. But I did think it would amuse the latter to hear his voice coming out of my mouth. Both actors are such marvellous old friends that I knew they would agree just to get me out of my predicament and help me get a little moolah to see me through my declining years.

Both wheezes were however still-born. Johnny Moff was busy night and day rehearsing and playing at our National Theatre and on the day planned for the post-syncing, Robert was called unexpectedly to work on a film for which he was contracted. So Mr Myers was on to me again. It so happened that the surgeon was in my room at the time in the Gordon Hospital (126 Vauxhall Bridge Road. Super nurses. Thick walls. Handy for visitors. Advt. And that's all you're going to be told about *my operation*, you'll be relieved to hear; I may go into my second one later!). Anyhow I asked my medical adviser if I could pop out of bed for a few hours the next day, do a not too strenuous job in a sitting position, help earn enough money to pay for *My Operation* and come back and hop into bed.

To my amazement (and, it must be confessed, dismay) he said 'Yes'. A car called for me the following morning and I slightly overplayed the part of the Brave Artiste enacting 'The Show Must Go On', or, in this case 'Commodore Bird's Eye Sails Again'.

I did feel very odd in the studio, though stoic. The trouble with my heroic effort was that, though for the first part of the session my voice was strong enough, it started to fade in the second. The results were not too catastrophic however and I 'improved' as they say in poker, at a repeat session a few weeks later. The rest is Fish Finger History.

For those who are interested in the financial aspect of the whole thing, I got five hundred quid for my trip to

Barbados and £1000 in residuals during the first few months. The fact that Commodore Bird's Eye seemed to have passed away had ceased to worry me and being the Voice of Kattomeat for so long was a considerable solace.

But, as you can imagine, this sort of emolument does unhinge one and when a few years later I was offered a cigar commercial, also in vision, I jumped for joy. This time I was to be paid 500 quid for *one* day's work at Shepperton Studios. We were to make a 'pilot' film for a possible series of commercials to promote a well-known tobacco firm's new small reasonably priced cigar.

Jim Clark, who had just had a big success with the first Marty Feldman film, was to direct and he'd had the brilliant idea of setting the commercial in a sort of '*Casablanca*' environment with clever John Bird in the Peter Lorre role and me as Sydney Greenstreet. It was a funny script and as usual we had a tip-top cameraman and crew.

Now the one snag about the whole operation was My Conscience. On 28 July 1963, just before the first of *Luther* at the Royal Court Theatre, I had made a bargain with God about Getting Me Through the first night. If He did, I said, I'd give up smoking from that moment on. It wasn't as much an act of self-sacrifice as you might think, as I was rapidly easing myself into the grave by an excess of coughing and retching around 9 o'clock every day. My period of smoking was between 6.30 and 9, when I was Facing the Foolscap and, after I'd disposed of over twenty cigarettes and begun my paroxysms, I hardly smoked at all the rest of the day.

I was terrified of *Luther*, as my part, although just a cameo in the second act, was what is called a 'tear off' and I knew it was important to my career not to get caught in a flurry of coughing or worse in the middle of my long speech. This is why I made my bargain. Anyhow He did get me through the evening and I gave up smoking just like *that* (Snap of the Fingers to be imagined). Since that day I have never been asked to play a part on stage, screen, television or, as a matter of fact, radio, which required me to smoke as Part of the Plot.

But here, with the proposed Player's Panama Cigar, was my first smoking assignment. I tried to convince my friends, myself and Him that this was different. To begin with, it was a cigar I was going to advertise, not a cigarette. That I had only smoked the latter in the past and that therefore the cigar didn't count as a Betrayal. In any case I would never touch the bloody things again. No, that's simply not true, as I write it I couldn't help hoping, in my most secret of hearts, that I would establish myself as The Fat Man in the P. Panama ads. As my Quest for Truth continued I tried to reason that I wasn't smoking for pleasure but it wasn't an attractive get-out. I also asked myself what I'd do if, in a play or a film, the director insisted on my smoking. But, of course, that's beside the point. And it was simply no good asking if He would insist on my keeping to my part of the bargain.

It was a tricky time and it would be bogus of me to pretend that I was ever really in any serious doubt as to what I *should* do. The fact remains that I did exactly the opposite and took the job. And don't think that I didn't secretly imagine that a chandelier would fall on my head or I'd catch fire during the day's shooting. But in fact it all went very smoothly, and seemingly successfully. I did get the most appalling nausea from smoking even one cigar, so you can imagine what I felt after smoking thirty-five supplied by the property department (not by Player's I hasten to add in case of libel).

We all sat back and awaited the outcome of our efforts. I went over to America to see about *The Teddy Bear Book* (whatever happened to that, by the way, I can hear you *not* asking) and was truly amazed to get back to England to find the most stupendous contract being drawn up to make a series of cigar commercials. I was to get a minimum of 5,000 quid for them and the possibilities were endless. They had options galore and who did I think I was to turn down such manna from heaven? The films were to be shot partly in Spain and the whole series wouldn't take longer than two weeks. It was Dreamsville plus. I postponed my usual odyssey to Greece, turned down a couple of jobs which I wouldn't have done anyhow and queried, through my agent, one or two minor *doubles entendres* in my contract.

Then the blow fell. I was told that the whole deal had been postponed because they hadn't (and I sort of quote because I was too shaken to remember the exact wording) found a suitable place to produce the product which they were proposing to promote viz: Player's Panama. Not quite enough P's in that last sentence are there?

It was the most bizarre excuse for not giving me 5,000 quid I could imagine but in a curious way I know that the location had nothing to do with it. Quite seriously I know I wasn't meant to do it but why the hand of God should also fall on the director and the remainder of the people concerned must remain a mystery.

Anyhow possibly before I have even finished re-typing this for the fourteenth time I shall find that it wasn't all a mirage and then the whole thing will be on the hob again and I shall be assailed by the same religious doubts. However we'll face that one when it surfaces.

And just before we return to the unhappy Teddy Bear saga, one more TV commercial story. Very recently of a Friday evening I was called by my agent and asked if I could do another 'pilot', this time for a new cheese under a famous brand name. It wasn't on anywhere near the scale of my previous 'visual' appearances and was just to 'show the client' what *could* be done. I was to get £45 and it could be shot on a Sunday which would suit me fine, as we don't open the shop on that particular day of the week. 'Forty-five pounds', I can hear you gasp in dismay. And you would be right. But, as I shall discuss in the last chapter of this book, the actor's salary has steadily fallen for the most part in the last few years, as a result of the fantastic level of unemployment in the profession.

Anyhoo the noo, with 'Kattomeat' slipping from between my fingers and only the fact of being a Cadbury's Fruit and Nut Case to keep my commercial morale up, I decided to cheese it. I did ask to see a script however and it was on my doorstep when I got home lateish the Friday night. The first line read 'A very idiosyncratic fat man with three chins is enthusiastically spreading bread, eating Blankety Blank Cheese throughout!' (Now I *am* being careful as it's Libel Fringe Time.)

Well I wasn't best pleased. For one thing I'd been on a diet for two months and lost two stone and therefore had only two chins, secondly I had mentioned that I couldn't possibly eat bread. Now Saturday is nowadays not the best day to find people in offices. After a fairly sleepless night I finally contacted one of the producers and told him that I didn't want to carry out my commitment under the circumstances. I mentioned to him that, apart from everything, I was so sylph like now, that I would spoil the chances of the commercial and gave him the names of several 'enormously fat men with three chins' (careful, Bull! No names, no packdrill! Whatever *that* means!)

He said the director would be getting in touch with him later in the day and that he would pass on the message. But in fact this never happened. A lady called me on Saturday evening to alter the time of my Sunday rendezvous and my previous pronunciamento burst on her astonished ears. The next call I got was from the director himself, who was apologetic, plausible, oozing with charm and had me in the studio the next morning after a very faint struggle. They (the Advertising Agency) had only been given the script after he'd called me, my size made no difference, he wanted me for my acting ability, etc., etc. You've no idea how *silly* actors are! You *must* have after all this.

Anyhow I didn't have to eat bread or butter but I did have to eat the cheese which was processed Cheddar. One of my lines was 'I never eat anything else these days. Most other Cheddars fall to pieces out of sheer tiredness by the time they get to the shop.'

I can only tell you that as my knife (in close-up) started cutting this fabulous new Cheddar it disintegrated into millions of fragments, which hardly fulfilled the promises of its blurb. By the end of the day we were sticking it together by every means, fair and mostly foul. I ate about 55 slices of the bloody stuff and ended by throwing up. But, as usual, the small unit were so enchanting that it was impossible to be cross, though I just wonder if this particular product will ever arrive intact at your local friendly store. I think this sort of commercial is really wicked, but just fulfilling the role of an actor connected with them, I hope, absolves me from complete culpability. But now let's get back to the dear little American Teddies, if you don't very much mind.

Now where were we? Oh yes, I see. Theodore was looking at *Life* (Magazine) and being thrilled with it all, little knowing what was in store for all of us. By March 1970 I had the dummy of the book in my hands. All that was left to do now was to caption the photographs and pray that there wouldn't be a further postponement. In order to make sure of this I took another trip at my own expense to New York at the end of April. (Disguised this time as a chrysanthemum grower.) It wasn't until I went over that autumn to promote the book that Random House put its tiny hand in its pocket. And truth to tell, they *needn't*, I suppose, even have done that.

Apart from the expense involved, this trip was satisfactory, and it really looked as if nothing could go wrong, but even as late as 25 May, publication date seems to have been set for 14 September. I did remonstrate a bit as, having waited so long, mid-October or the beginning of November seemed to me a more likely date to catch the full impact of Christmas trade. This battle I won before leaving.

I had a lovely holiday in Greece, with a lot of encouraging letters from Jean Ennis about her publicity plans. These included sending small Steiff Teddies to all the reviewers, despite the Steiff Public Relations representative refusing to cooperate on the grounds that I was biased in the book about his firm's part in the origin of the T. Bear. Jean was very keen on a party in the Smithsonian Institute in Washington to celebrate the publication day as it is there that the original Teddy Bear is supposed to be housed.

In September of 1970 I got my advance copies of the book and it is here that I must say that it was a thrilling job. Beautifully printed on sepia throughout, the whole thing (apart from the aforementioned snap of me on the back) was well-nigh perfect. Sally Kovalchick and the Art Dept had done a superb job, and with their help and a bit of luck I don't think anyone else will be producing a book on the subject of Teddy Bears for a century or so.

I flew to America on 13 October 1970 and it's the only time that I've considered that the number 13 possibly carries unlucky implications. By the way, harking back a bit, you should have seen the looks on my crew's faces when we sailed for the disastrous Dieppe raid and I received instructions to paint that number on our bows. But in that case we were lucky to return unscathed.

The book was due to come out on the 19th and, after considerable thought, dear Jean Ennis had decided not to have a great party. She had lined up an impressive list of TV shows, radio ditto's, and so we were just going to have a little celebration lunch of our own. I called her on the morning of publication day to make arrangements about time and place to rendezvous and, to my surprise, she wasn't in her office. I kept on phoning and her frightfully efficient British secretary, Ann Senior, finally got so worried that she went to Jean's flat. After banging on the door, the porter finally got in, to discover that Jean had died of a heart attack during the week-end.

So from the outset everything seemed fated. She had always been my staunchest supporter and, without her interest at the start, the whole idea would have been still-born. Poor gentle Jean. Her death shattered us all and there was a particularly gloomy Memorial service, which I know she would have loathed. Luckily for me, Ann Senior proved able to continue Jean's work on my behalf, and, because she knew more than anyone else in the Publicity office about the whole project, she was assigned to me throughout the whole of the promotion. She and Sally got on very well together and without their love for the book and completely unphoney attachment for me, we would have had complete disaster on our hands.

For one thing, I had hoped that Random House would have secured permission for me to work on TV for the entire period of my stay. I had already had trouble during previous visits with the Immigration authorities who are nearly as difficult with British artistes as we are with Americans. But the fact remains that, if an actor is by some happy chance given a visa to perform on Broadway or act in a film in Hollywood, it is hell's own job getting a *Paid* TV show, unless he (or she) is a zonking great star and it's not always easy then.

In theory I only had a working visa to do shows during the first week of publication, including the Dick Cavett show, which is (or certainly was then) the most influential of all the talk shows. I had appeared on his show once before and I thought I'd made rather a muck of things, but this time all was well. I followed the singer Neil Diamond and Hugh Downs, who, himself an interviewer, was the gent who had brought forth a tremendous response when he'd had me on his show some years previously and asked viewers to send me letters and information about Teddy Bears.

Dick Cavett treated me very civilly and, unlike so many of the hosts I had to cope with later on my tour, didn't send the whole thing up rotten. He had even read (or certainly looked at) the book itself which is more than can be said for some of the others. I was followed by the Governor of the Arkansas prison, who was closely cross-questioned by Mr C. about all the sinister mounds which had been discovered littering the place and subsequently turned out to be unidentified burial grounds. I thanked heaven that I had had my say before this particularly chilly interview, and not after it.

Anyhow I gathered from Random House that I had gone well enough to get a favourable response from all over the country and various talk shows, who had hesitated before, now decided to engage me. Over there the procedure is totally different from here and it's only on the big shows you get paid, and never on radio. I did masses of the latter and I greatly enjoyed most of them. By the way I got $265 for the Cavett show, which was not to be sneezed at. I was getting only minimal expenses from Random House but it was I who chose to remain in the country for over two months with a brief holiday in Tobago bang in the middle of the exploitation. It must be confessed that Random House paid all my expenses when on tour but New York was my own financial responsibility. Luckily I have a tiny pad there, in the shape of a small room in the huge flat of a Teddy Bear owner I know, called Ronnie Monroe. In fact it was to his Teddy Bear (T. Edward) I dedicated my book. I took T. Edward with me on tour and he became quite a TV personality on his own account.

The next New York TV show I was required for was 'Tell the Truth'. This is a show where three people are assembled from ordinary walks of life and one of them is chosen to be the principal contestant. The other two pretend to be him (or her) and a panel of TV personalities ask them questions to decide which is the genuine article. It is a real audience participation show and anyone can write in and appear on it. Like 'What's My Line?' it has been going on almost since TV was invented and there is no question of either show ever ending. In America they are both the property of Goodson-Todman enterprises and I got to know Mr Goodson rather well as he turned out to be one of my fellow contestants.

As I had foreseen I was to be disguised but I hadn't

expected to wear a Teddy Bear skin with Mr Goodson similarly attired. The third member of our little group was my friend Tom Poston, whom I had supported when he starred in a film called *The Old Dark House*. The droll thing about his appearance as a Teddy Bear in 'Tell the Truth' was the fact that he was a regular member of the panel of the same game. I think he submitted to the indignity, to say nothing of the discomfort, because he was a chum of mine. Anyhow it was all great fun and we all did our respective imitations of Noel Coward to confuse the panel. Mine was easily the worst so they guessed it was me right away to the huge delight of Mr Goodson, who I suspect is an actor manqué instead of being an immensely successful producer.

For my appearance in the show I was awarded a Samsonite Attaché Case and a wig, both of which came in extremely useful. The producers of the show put in a bid to the Immigration people for my (and I quote) 'unique services', which may have helped my not being pursued quite as relentlessly as I could have been, though permission was only given to do this one show. In the meantime I was going round all the principal bookstores in New York, chatting up the buyers, salesladies, signing copies and carrying out the same routine, which I'd done so often in London.

On 1 November I flew off on the first of my tourettes or bijou tours. First stop the dreaded Detroit, where I had had so many traumatic experiences with *Pickwick*. I did a TV show, which apparently was not to be shown until Christmas, owing to the pressure of political upheaval in the city at the time. I was fortunate to get away that night and go straight to Cincinatti where I was to appear on a TV programme called 'The Parsley, Sage, Jani and Love Show' (believe it or not).

This turned out to be quite a hoot as Jani Gardner was an immensely attractive young lady who makes quite a living out of little books called *How to Seduce Your Husband in 365 Different Ways* and that sort of thing. Her interview spot was in two halves. The first was straight and the second was where the guest did a cooking spot. I had been warned about this and, when Jani asked me what I was going to do, I said 'Make an English Cup Of Tea', she said it wouldn't take the full quarter of an hour allocated. I said it would the way I made an English Cup of Tea.

It had to be a proper dish she said and I forebore to make the obvious crack and settled on kedgeree, at which I am unbeatable and of which Miss Gardner had never heard. However all the ingredients were at hand in a trice though the smoked haddock didn't look exactly as I had remembered it. Nathless once we were 'on the air' I set to work as professionally as I could and it all seemed as easy as pie (fish).

The last twelve minutes of 'The Parsley, Sage, Jani and Love Show' opened with us eating my recipe and this is where we nearly lost the Jani part of the show. I just managed to stop her putting a forkful of kedgeree into her mouth which contained the largest bone in my culinary history. 'Oh I'm most frightfully sorry,' I said, 'but I seem to have forgotten to take the bones out.' After that Miss Gardner ate slowly and with caution but I think very few Cincinatti housewives would be trying out my recipe if and when the recording was finally shown. I got $165, which is the highest fee I've ever earned for making kedgeree.

It was in Cincinatti that I was first conscious of the lack of cooperation or liaison between the Sales Dept of Random House and the local bookstores. I had been scheduled to go to a signing session in Shillatoes, the biggest store there, but *malheureusement* there wasn't a single copy for me to put my name to. Five hundred were air-freighted the next day by mistake (they ordered 50), but by that time I was in Chicago.

In Windy City as it's called I had a lovely and, on the whole, successful time. I was shepherded from studio to studio and bookstore to bookstore by a formidable lady called Dorothy Strong. She was frightfully efficient and extremely nice. She had organized every minute of my five days there and I did everything except stand on my head. I appeared with my Teddies at a fashion show and with Jacques Cousteau, Piper Laurie (remember *her*?) on the Kup show, which is the top Chicago TV programme and for which you aren't paid a sausage, though you are given a Kup's Kup with your name inscribed on it, which I suppose is something.

By now I was getting rather adept at the job and as a result a bit cheeky. The interviewers I took an instant dislike to were the ones who hadn't even bothered to take the book out of the cellophane wrapping. 'Waal, Mr Bull,' they used to say cheerfully, 'I haven't had time to look at your book but ...' and I found myself saying courteously, 'Oh but you must. We've got plenty of time now.' And take it out of their hands and show it them with a sweet smile. 'Isn't it beautifully got up?' I would say, and they had to agree with murder in their eyes and heart.

Then there were the ones who *had* looked at the book and thrown up. 'Mr Bull, don't you think it a bit childish to collect Teddy Bears?' I used to pause and then say, as if after deep thought, 'I don't really think it's much more childish than collecting yachts, motor-cars or wives. After all they are an extraordinary race. They've done practically everything. For instance they've climbed the Matterhorn.' Pause. 'When did *you* last climb the Matterhorn?' 'They've broken every speed record on land and sea. Or rather Sir Donald Campbell's Mr Woppit did. They've saved children's lives. Saved any children's lives recently, Mr Blank?' I only reserved the last shot if they were really beastly to me.

But by this time I was shameless about the whole thing. I carried the oldest and most valuable Teddies in two bags with their heads showing out of the top. Teddies get claustrophobia just as much as humans. And before *you* throw up, I have to report one of the bags they travelled in had imprinted on the front in letters of gold 'E. Bear Esq.' Oh you *have* thrown up, have you? Bad luck!

It was fun taking them on the plane, particularly in the almost empty Jumbo Jets, to which Random House so generously treated us on the long flights. I would put the

Senior Citizen Teddies on the seat beside me and when the Air Hostess passed, ask her to fasten their safety belts please. Quite often she'd panic and dash off to the Captain's cabin to report that they had a prospective hijacker on board and that the little dears probably had revolvers concealed about their persons. But usually they were terribly sweet and made a tremendous fuss of them, bringing them special meals, toys, etc., which they appreciated enormously.

But enough of this whimsy. Around this time almost every Sunday newspaper in the country ran a five- to six-page story about the book and me in their coloured supplement. I personally think *this* was the moment when Random *should* have been thinking of a possible reprint but more of that later. We were, it is true, still six weeks off Christmas. Miss Strong did a terrific job for me in Chicago and the newspaper columns were full of the bears. I met a lot of delightful people there and visited one of my favourite arctophilists, Miss Dinah Cody, who has a Bear House in her sitting-room which is quite astonishing. The bears have their own TV, there are practical cooking and washing-up appliances in the kitchen and all the bathrooms are the same. Theodore was put in the spare room to rest, while we had dinner, after a tumultuous welcome. When we arrived at her apartment house, there was a small red carpet running up the stairs and the door was wide open with her entire collection of Teddies waving banners which read 'Theodore for President' and various other slogans. I tried to respond regally to this reception starting off 'Theodore and I'.

Los Angeles was not such an easy nut to crack. I was able though to see a great deal of some of my best friends and Tab Hunter, with whom I was staying, threw a magnificent party for me, about which beautiful downtown Burbank, where it was held, is reported to be still talking. Gathered together for the occasion were an astonishing mixture of the horsey set (Tab is the uncrowned king of them), the famous and the notorious. But I think we all had a wonderful time and the Teddies had their friends along and what went on in Tab's stables during the evening is anybody's guess.

In Hollywood a gentleman called Jay Allen looked after me like a Nanny. As I've said in another portion of this book, it is death not to be on wheels in the Tinsel City and though my hosts were kind enough to act as chauffeurs while I was there, it was Jay who had to bear the responsibility of getting me from place to place.

I couldn't get on any of the really big shows in Hollywood so had to content myself with the Steve Allen one, which used to be very high in the ratings but has slipped considerably. And I could quite see why, when I saw the inefficiency of the production side and the total lack of any contact with Mr Allen before the show. This engagement incidentally almost led to litigation as only actors are paid for appearing on it and authors and suchlike, promoting their works, are expected to give their services free.

However AFTRA (Associated Federation of Television and Radio Artistes, I think), of which I am still a member, insisted that I *must* be paid or I'd be expelled from their union, and, after a great deal of haggling, I got my moolah. But apart from a delightfully pixilated correspondent of the *Los Angeles Times*, I had a thin time publicity-wise. This gentleman thanked me for 'bringing beauty to Hollywood' and went all the way in a most gratifying manner.

Then on my last hop of this particular junket to beautiful San Francisco, which seemed curiously unchanged since my last visit, just 32 years previously. That time Bob Morley and I were playing truant from working in a film called *Marie Antoinette*, in the final version of which you could just see my right elbow if you looked closely. However I was in Hollywood for six months and put a play of Mr Morley's on in London on the proceeds.

Here again I was in clover, digs-wise, staying with friends I had known and loved for a long time, in an apartment high above the bay with a super view of the Golden Gate. There were very few TV studios in the city but the shows

I did do were warm and friendly, like the city, and I had a ravishing time on a Children's Christmas programme.

And then it was back to New York for my photo session with *Life* magazine, which proved such a wash-out for Theodore and me, as already reported. I was quite exhausted by the tour and delighted that I was taking a week off. You see, in America, television starts around six in the morning and the theory, which is probably and horrifyingly true, is that the Great American Public is at its most vulnerable peak early in the morning. In any case the TV is turned on at rising and kept running, while shaving, bathing, eating breakfast, and up to the moment of leaving the building. It is only actually viewed when there is something which interests the person concerned and quite often steps are taken to buy the book, see the play or film, or get the article which is mentioned. Whereas in the evening, relaxed and half asleep at home, there is less chance of remembering A Thing the following day.

After an idyllic week in Tobago it was off on the treadmill again. First stop Cleveland. This city, like Detroit, is full of unhappy Pickwickian memories but this time it wasn't so fearsome.

I have very happy memories of an open line radio show I did there. This is the sort which allows anyone to phone in and ask questions and in Cleveland we had some humdingers. Like the lady who asked me to stop talking about Teddy Bears for heaven's sake. She told me that she was sick of the bloody things. I asked why and she said that her husband still took his to bed every night and she hated the feel of it. She then told me that they'd been married thirty years.

It was about now that I found out that copies of my book were simply not in evidence in 75 per cent of the stores to whom they had apparently been sent. As Random House were paying for my tour the whole thing seemed pretty senseless. I pressed on to Detroit, where the position in the shops was even worse. I did a very early morning TV show and was due to appear on an important Radio programme called 'Focus' in the Fisher Building where so many traumas connected with *Pickwick* had taken place a few years before. I might have guessed something would go wrong there. I met the producer who told me that a Miss Gloria Swanson had decided at the last moment to appear on the programme, as she was playing down below at the Fisher Theater in *Butterflies are Free* and was, it was rumoured, not packing the building.

Waaaaaal, as I am sure they say somewhere in America, she was first on and that was it. She talked about macrobiotics and compost until we practically smelt the stuff. Not a word about Pola Negri, leopard cubs, Valentino or Eric Von Stroheim, just pure manure throughout. I couldn't get a word in edgeways nor indeed could the interviewer. At about two minutes before the close of the programme, the latter said, 'Thank you, Miss Swanson. I am afraid we have had no time to discuss Peter Bull's delightful and witty *Teddy Bear Book*. Good-bye folks.' All the way to Detroit to get that sort of thing. Miss Swanson opened those wide eyes of hers and, flashing them at me, said, 'Oh, I'm so sorry, I thought it was only me on the programme.' How could one be angry with such a lady? I was *livid*.

On to Minneapolis where at any rate I was in congenial company, staying with my friend Chuck Nolte, the original Billy Budd in the play of that name, and now a fully fledged Professor of Drama in the University of Minnesota. Apart from the usual story at the bookshops 'We've been waiting a week for fresh supplies' it was a pleasant enough time and then it was back to New York, for a fresh onslaught on fame and fortune and if possible to shake Random House to their foundation. I achieved none of these. But I did do 'What's My Line?'

Then it was time for 'Philadelphia Here I Come' and that was the most disastrous trip of all. To begin with, I *had* been going by 'The Metroliner', which is a sensationally fast puffer-train and it was the only time I'd even thought of using this mode of transport. I'd booked my seat and all and it was supposed to get you there in under one and a half hours. On *that* day the Railway had a token strike. So it was out to the airport which takes about an hour, if the traffic's terrible, and ditto the other end. I got there in time to give a newspaper interview, after which I strolled round to Wannamaker's, the main store, where the head of the book department said he'd been waiting three weeks for copies. Random House incidentally had smothered him in other books. As *Life* had just come out with it's four-page spread and I was on general release doing 'What's My Line?' and the Steve Allen show, it all seemed lunacy. And not a copy in Gimbels, the other big shop. However I pressed on to see the worst show I'd ever seen, in order to cheer me up. I had heard it was having trouble on the road and I'm afraid I'd always rather see a really awful show than a medium one. Mark you, I still like the best sort best, but I had already seen that one, *No No Nanette*, which was the only alternative in Philadelphia that particular night.

What I did see was a musical version of *Exodus* called *Ari* and it started off with a Concentration Camp Ballet. Get the picture? I hugged myself and the rest of the evening was equally hilarious. Every time a child died of starvation, the hero and the heroine burst into song and it lasted just two weeks when it got to New York. Afterwards I did a radio show in the restaurant of the hotel where I was staying though the audience, I think rightly, preferred to eat and drink rather than listen. I can't pretend it was one of my major triumphs.

It was about now that I realized I'd shot my bolt and anyhow I'd planned to be back in England for Christmas. No-one else seemed to want my services and I was obviously a pest to Random House. But Washington was the one place I still hadn't visited and there was news value I fancied in a trip there. We planned 14 December as a Good Day. I wanted to visit the Original Teddy Bear in the Smithsonian and there was a mad idea that Alice Roosevelt

Longworth might see me. This formidable lady, in her eighties, is still the social leader of the Capitol and will not suffer fools gladly. She is also the daughter of Theodore Roosevelt, after whom the bear is named. Dear Ann Senior who had taken over from Jean Ennis bravely phoned to ask quite simply if I could present a copy of the book to her. I think she sensed there was an ulterior motive because she hedged. She wouldn't fix definitely on the Monday we planned but demanded that I rang her on that morning. It was curious (a) how easily we got hold of her phone number and (b) how she always seemed to answer in person.

We decided to take a chance and I asked the new head publicity lady if I could take Ann with me. After a certain amount of haggling I got my wish. We arrived nice and early and I phoned Mrs Longworth on arrival. She said I could come to tea as long as I didn't bring (a) any member of the press or (b) any Teddy Bears. By the tone in which she spoke I couldn't make out which she disliked the thought of most. I thought it inadvisable even to take Ann and spent the rest of the day in Abject Terror.

However it was off to the Smithsonian Museum first and after signing innumerable security papers, and practically being stripped, we were shown into an office, where eventually the Original Teddy Bear was produced, which I fear is an impostor. Everything about him suggests the twenties and he has none of the signs of age which the Teddies of the early part of the century show only too clearly. It was indeed presented (can't even bring myself to call it a 'he') to the Roosevelt family by Mr Michtom of Ideal Toys, who are supposed to be the originators of the whole thing, but, I fear it can only have been a publicity stunt, and it or he can sue me if it or he likes. No wonder it isn't on show but kept quietly under surveillance. My own bear Theodore gave it the Thumbs Down the moment he saw it. I hadn't dared to tell him yet that he wasn't going to be allowed to meet Mrs Longworth and would have to remain concealed in my pocket.

Naturally I didn't say a word to the Smithsonian gentlemen. It wasn't my business. Neither is it my business to tell you that the original Winnie the Pooh was destroyed by a dog and the animal who appeared at the Victoria and Albert Museum recently in the Ernest Shepard exhibition was not, according to the artist, the Original Pooh at all. How's that for a sensational bit of information?

After we'd unmasked the phoney Teddy Bear in the Smithsonian we visited a few bookshops, where, it must be instantly admitted, there were several copies of my book, which perked us up a bit. A dainty lunch with an old friend of mine (readers of the 'Pickwick' saga will perhaps remember her as the lady with the Praying Mantis) and then I pressed on alone to tea with Alice Roosevelt Longworth.

She lives in a solid, splendidly Edwardian mansion and, when I arrived, she was just finishing resting. One of her young relatives was there to greet me and luckily we had a lot in common as she had just returned from a holiday in Corfu and knew a lot of the people I'd come into contact with. Mrs Longworth came in later and was as cosy as could be. We had muffins from a silver dish, she disclaimed all knowledge of her father having started the Teddy Bear cult, loathed Teddies herself, accepted my book gracefully, talked wittily about George V's Coronation which she'd attended, the hideous hotel they'd erected next door to her house, the theatre—and I had a marvellous afternoon. She even asked me to visit her again and I felt like Judas because I couldn't tell her that I was meeting a posse of writers from the *Washington Post* immediately afterwards to tell them how it had all gone.

Well, we made the front page in one of the papers and *Time* magazine again and so the visit was well worth while. Back in New York the next day I did a final tour of the bookshops. It was still nearly two weeks to Christmas and the Ideal Christmas Gift was hardly anywhere to be seen owing to shortage of supplies at the publishers'. The week before we had apparently sold 1500 copies at $10 apiece and out of those I was hoping to get $1 for every one. It was really heartbreaking. I stormed Random House and actually managed by chance to see the president, Bob Bernstein, who listened sympathetically. Jim Silberman did ditto and, after I'd given him my report on the tour and general conditions, sent me back a denial of most of the facts, supplied by the Sales Dept. It was compiled a week or so after my complaint and, by that time, probably copies had trickled through, but nothing like the number in demand. There was no question of getting the reprint through till February 1971, by which time the impact of all the publicity would be as dead as Christmas.

It is still incomprehensible that, with a book like that, they should have underprinted. It could obviously sell reasonably well every Christmas. And yet during the following one (1972) no special effort was made to promote it though I was touched by a small toy shop on Second Avenue having its entire window devoted to bears and copies of my book. 1973 has been much better, I will admit, and the book was seen by Mr R. Morley in Brentano's window.

But earlier in the year a Random House financial statement came in, from which I found that about $1000 had been deducted from my royalty earnings, because in their belated attempts to distribute the book RH had sold large quantities to people they call 'jobbers' ('wholesalers' to us). These gentlemen have apparently to be propitiated with enormous discounts before they will buy any book, and by my contract I received only a reduced royalty on such sales. What I could not see was why the author had to suffer in this case, having lost several thousands of dollars through what looked like sheer inefficiency in failing to send the books out in proper time to the regular bookstores.

The fascinating thing was that when I remonstrated, dear old Random House decided to split the difference between what I would have received if the 'jobbers' hadn't been called in and what I did in fact get on the first royalty return. My astute agent advised me to say 'Snap' before they changed their mind.

And that's that, as far as *The Teddy Bear Book* is concerned. Curiously enough I'm not bitter about it all, though I know I sound it. The point being that it looked superb and I was proud of it. I met and have remained friends with two out of three of my editors. I owe unbounded gratitude to both of them, namely Steven Aronson and Sally Kovalchick. And the same goes for the late Jean Ennis and the very present Ann Senior; and I shall be wiser next time I get caught up in the machinery of a vast publishing organization. At worst I gleaned a random harvest from Random House and if the finished product had not been so professional, we should all have looked pretty silly. And I did after all get to appear in 'The Parsley, Sage, Jani and Love Show'.

V

LIFE IS STILL A CUCUMBER, I HOPE

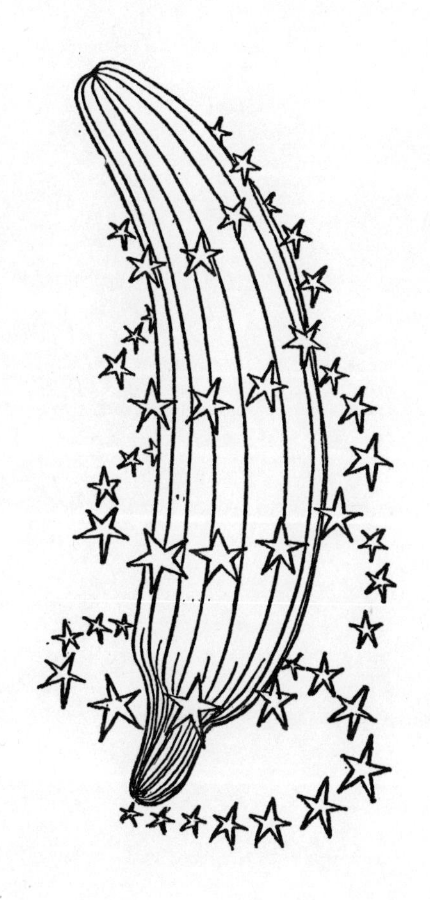

12. *Look to the Stars*

As readers of *Tit Bits, Harper's Bazaar, Screw* magazine, *Vogue*, the *Kensington Post, Reveille* and TV viewers of 'The David Dimbleby Talk-In' have realized, with my sincere gratitude to these institutions, I am now a partner in an Astrological Emporium called 'Zodiac' at the Notting Hill Gate end of Kensington Church St. I suppose I've always wanted to play at shops since I was about six years old and it is fortunate that in the 'tea-time of life' as my father called it, I have been able to realize my dream. Luckily my partner, Don Busby, doesn't 'Play at it' otherwise I think we would be out of business by now.

Originally I wanted to combine it with some Gipsy Tea Rooms and who knows but that I won't again strike lucky and, handsomely attired and backed up by a small ladies' band, be dispensing crumpets and raspberry jam, anchovy toast and home-made cakes to all and sundry. Particularly sundry. Thrown in will be a first-class tea-cup reading by our staff ('resting' actors and actresses thinly disguised as wandering gipsies). I think this is just what London is clamouring for. Mark you, I think people will be so mad about the idea that there will be a danger of them outstaying their welcome in which case I shall have parking meters by the tables so that the occupants can stay as long as they like if they pay extra.

Then I suppose we should have to hire a Labrador to sniff out the pot-smokers as I gather dogs of this breed are better at that sort of thing than police gentlemen and anyhow the presence of one of the latter in Gipsy Tea Rooms wouldn't help the atmosphere I am hoping to create. But what fun it all *could* be. We'd do a sort of computerized horoscope so that we could have tables specially allocated to the two signs most suited to each other that day. I want to make it quite clear that we wouldn't be starting a knocking-shop or anything like that, but we all know that it's love that makes the world go round and if we can put an astrological slant on it, so much the better. And who knows but that we might not induce some lovely star to appear briefly to play the violin to a gramophone record and disappear so quickly that the beholders would think it was all a mirage. Dear Harry Secombe has been approached and announced his willingness to participate.

But all this will have to wait until I can find proper premises. The snag all along has been that it is almost impossible to get a brand new 'Catering Licence' for premises which haven't had it before, and it has been impossible to persuade local councils that there will be no cooking, except of accounts and crumpets. 'Ah,' but they expostulate, 'how do we know that you won't turn into a fish and chips shop?' I tell them in a haughty voice that it is extremely unlikely and keep on thinking of the way Beatrice Lillie says 'Me, wot's always 'ad me own 'orses'. So that's that. When we came across this little building in Kensington Mall we knew it was right to buy it. There was a Teddy Bear in the corner of the top room, for starters. The whole place was in the peak of condition and as pretty as paint. The people who owned it were dears. They asked a lot, we agreed and, compared with the sort of stuff we had been seeing, it was a bargain.

For several months we'd been on the search and were

'gazumped' out of a building in Pimlico Road, on which we'd rather set our hearts. But it was possibly a stroke of luck that it happened, as our current home has a happier atmosphere about it and is ideal for the purpose. If only you could have seen some of the premises we were offered. Even the Estate Agents reeled back at the pong as we entered a lot of them. They obviously had never set foot in them and the floor was littered with bills for the last four tenants; one would never have had a quiet moment, what with the drains, and the writ-servers outnumbering the customers by at least two to one.

We were originally thinking of letting the flat upstairs to Russian spies as I got rather windy when we thought of how much we owed the bank. Also it'd be fun when they were arrested (it's v. near the Embassy) to say 'They were just ordinary people like you and me', to the reporters and/or Mrs Bingham, if she was around. But if we did this we realized that (a) we should have to put a loo in the shop below, because of Staff Regulations Article 2384 or something (b) we would have had to hire one of the garages opposite for extra storage and (c) we would never be able to cook anything for ourselves. So we live above the premises on and off and it's all very cosy with Georgina, our palmist, in a room on the first floor, about whom more anon.

It's only since our brave decision that we've also found out, that if we *had* let the flat above there would have been nowhere to sit down and the whole thing would have been hell. Quite apart from having to put bugging devices into the flat to catch the Russian spies at it, if you know what I mean. So now we've got the best of both possible worlds, a thing I always think very worth while.

Mark you, I couldn't have undertaken the shop without D. Busby, who is a Leo and as tough as old boots. It was he who calmly announced many months before we had opened or even found premises, that he was off to Blackpool. As he had never been north of Golders Green before I was impressed. 'Why?' I asked. 'The Blackpool Gift Fair,' he announced. 'Of course,' I said, having never heard of the thing. So off he trotted, spent three days there, commuting from Manchester as Blackpool was full of the 20,000 traders who visit it at that time of year and back he came with assorted specimens, all to do with the Zodiac. He accumulated stock like a squirrel nuts and it was fascinating watching an American make himself quite so much at home in our grey and fairly pleasant land.

As I was still, and in a way still am, planning the Gipsy Tea Rooms, I let him run the shop. I am treated as a sort of cretinous tea lady and when I'm the Mailing Department, which is quite often, I am not really trusted to do up a Fortune Tea Cup (60p plus 17p for postage and a bargain at that), but I love dealing with the actual mail. It's fun to me to bring back courtesy into relationships with customers. I start off letters with 'Your esteemed order' or 'Your kind enquiry' and end up 'Assuring you of our best attention always, I remain your obedient servant' which, I imagine, hits them between the eyes. I know sudden politeness, like a bus actually stopping at a Request Stop when one holds up one's hand, or somebody holding a door open for me in Boots The Cash Chemists, is apt to reduce me to tears. Anyhow Courtesy is our Watchword. And, as for the customers who come into the shop, let them wander round as long as they like. Let them read whole books, as long as they don't break the backs of same, feel all the Tarot cards etc. and then not buy anything, with a sweet smile we say 'Thank You' as they leave the building in such a way that either they return forthwith or break their bloody necks on the step out of sheer surprise.

Oh yes, I'm very keen on proving that I come from a nation of shopkeepers and am getting pretty ruthless at the job. Don't think I don't fill all the Zodiac piggy-banks with a half p so that the children can hear them rattle. The other day a patently rich lady brought her very difficult six-year-old in to 'buy a present for Daddy'. She kept on, to our delight, showing him the more expensive gifts in our shop.

The kiddiwink expressed extreme boredom and thumbed down the lot. I slid along with one of our most expensive crystal goblets. 'Do you think,' I said to the child in my most cooing voice, 'Daddy would like this for his toothbrush?' And that was six quid in the kitty without much pain. Oh I do hope this isn't putting you off visiting us.

The trouble with writing a book like this is that, what with strikes, to say nothing of the stress of living, it is impossible to predict what will be happening by the time this book is actually published. For all I know, I may have taken up landscape gardening but, come what may, I think the Astrological Emporium will be sitting there, in its bright blue and yellow colours. Everyone asks me how we came to think of it. After all it's the first shop of its kind in Britain. And I don't know if my answer is satisfactory enough. Some years ago, I was given by Mr and Mrs André Morell (Joan Greenwood to you) a most lovely black and gold Portmerion mug. It was in Aries natch (as I happen to have been born on the First Day of Spring) and the thing was that I was shortly leaving for America and I couldn't think of anything I'd really like to take more as presents for my friends. Leo and Capricorn were what I lusted after and could I find them at any of the stores who stocked these particular mugs? Not on your nelly! Can that last phrase be right? It looks peculiar from where I'm sitting.

Anyhow my friends had to go without that visit but when Don Busby came over from the States to live and we were playing about with the idea of an Astrology shop, I did think it would be rather nice if we could have a complete stock of every sign. Now then, don't all come rushing along the moment you read this because my theory had one fatal flaw. No, two. Transport and availability of material. We order crystal eggs from Sweden and the damned things lie about in docks for months and in Britain work on crystal glass was practically suspended for several months except for goods which featured the silver wedding of Our Gracious Queen. Another astonishing factor is that there is no doubt that certain signs sell better than others. Virgo people have a reputation for being 'picky' (they would describe themselves as perfectionists) so we don't sell as many of them. No Cancerian is v. keen on their sign and Scorpio people are impulsive and prefer the glyph of their sign on jewellery rather than the actual animal. My dears, the things I've learned since the shop opened.

Aries persons (like me) keep on hitting their heads and it is absolutely true. My partner, Mr Busby, can spot them practically before they have gone round the shop, because of their impulsive behaviour. It's the same with handwriting. We have some rather chic visitors' books upstairs where our friends sign their names and put their date of birth (not year as the ladies aren't all that keen, to say nothing of some of the gents). You'd be *amazed* at the results, when you view a whole page of these Visiting Sheets. Aries write very small and Sagittarians very big and seem to be colossal show-offs (they write messages in Greek or Hebrew and that sort of thing). The Cancer lot follow the spacing of the person above, exactly like sheep, whereas the Librans *have* to balance things, and, if there is an empty space on a page, they leap in there. Scorpio's have flashy signatures with big capitals and Taurus handwriting is firm and stolid.

Now I've noticeably got less and less sceptical since we opened and, I assure you, it's not for financial (or even publicity) reasons. You see, so many extraordinary things have happened. For instance the lady wot does horoscopes who suddenly came into our lives. I came bouncing into the shop one morning and this lady hands me My Natal Chart. And for those of you who know nothing about the subject, an N.C. is a geometrical expression of the planetary tendencies at the time you were born. In order to make it valid, the exact time and place are required, as longitude and latitude have to be allowed for in calculations.

So I thanked the nice lady and asked her how the hell she knew when I was born.

'It's on Page One of *Bulls in the Meadows*,' she replied

sweetly. And that *was* a conversation stopper. A few days later she sent me my entire horoscope. It was extremely well-observed and there were conclusions drawn, for which she could not have had a clue. I called her up to thank her. Her name is Joyce Sanderson by the way. She then announced that she'd done a horoscope of the shop. I did chortle a bit at that one and got a well-deserved rebuke from the other end of the blower.

'If you know the date of birth of a seemingly inanimate object, it's perfectly easy to plan a chart for it,' she said severely. 'Why on earth did you open on May 1st? All the signs were against it. Did something dreadful happen that day?'

I had to admit that the sign-writer hadn't finished his work by the time we opened and a ladder was firmly poised against the front door for the whole of the morning. This kept the superstitious customers away. However Joyce assured me that 'Zodiac's' dear little chart showed an unbroken line of success from that moment on except for one thing. I asked her what.

It seemed that there was danger of fire. At this I nearly dropped the phone. The day before there had been a fire at the back of the shop next door and I'd had to call the fire brigade. As Joyce lives in Essex she couldn't have seen it or indeed heard of it but our building was slightly singed and I bought a fire extinguisher next day. But it's the combination of coincidences which are too strong to ignore. If I started telling you of some of our palmist's successes you wouldn't believe them. And it's not that she told us (palmists take a kind of hippocratic oath like doctors) but her clients would come whirring down from her room amazed and bewildered by her E.S.P.—The conjuring up of an exact portrait of a loved one or an aspect of a career about which only the client knew.

She has been a great asset to the shop and it is fascinating to me the way you can always tell the people who are sceptical and yet want a go. They shuffle round the shop pretending to look at the books and other goods, but waiting for the shop to be empty. Then there is usually this conversation:

'Do you believe in all this sort of stuff?'

'As a matter of fact I do,' I reply.

'Oh, I don't. I think it's all a lot of cods wallop, rubbish, balls' (according to the type of speaker).

Silence.

'*You* don't believe in this palmist stuff do you?'

'Yes.'

'Extraordinary.' Fingering of the palmist's card goes on.

'Well I don't. But she isn't by chance free now, is she? You see I've got this problem and, though I've made up my mind, I'd like a second opinion.' And that's that. They're hooked on it and in nine cases out of ten, they come down beaming and contented.

We also have attached to us an Astrologer, a Graphologist, a Tarot Card reader, quite apart from dear Mrs Sanderson, who has appointed herself Court Consultant and won't take a penny for all the work she puts in, settling our future hashes.

Not content with starting on an astrological career, I have also got involved in the Ladies' Literary Lunch circuit, which, by the time this book has been published, I shall probably have left. So then I can afford to be fairly indiscreet. Only fairly, just in case I want jam on my bread and butter.

Whereas I've practically had to give up acting owing to nerves and the general tension which surrounds the world of entertainment nowadays (a specified Whining and Grizzling passage is coming up in the next section), I don't mind the improvised part of it all. I don't mean I like pretending I am a tree or a piece of parsley, I mean it's not difficult for me to say the first words which come into my head. Whereas proper actors hate the TV talk shows and it scares the daylights out of them even to open a bazaar, I really rather thrive on that sort of thing and, when Cyril Fletcher asked me if I'd like to become part of his circus called 'Associated Speakers', I said yes with alacrity before he changed his mind.

Now all you have to do to be an Associated Speaker is to get up fairly early in the morning from time to time and take a railway train out of London to some other city. The clubs pay your first class fare and so it's a question of whipping into the loo with your second class ticket just before arrival at your destination and pocketing the extra money later, when your cheque is discreetly handed to you. The loo deception is just in case the secretary of the club is bold enough to come on the platform. One of the secretaries did try and fob me off with second class expenses on the grounds that I was a friend of her son's. I told her, through Associated Speakers, that it was unlikely that I would remain his friend, if I didn't get my first class ticket. So *that* was all right.

On arrival at your destination you are met by the secretary of the club or one of her deputies and usually driven straight to the rendezvous where, at first sight, the room seems just full of hats. One has sort of forgotten that people wear hats any more but Ladies' Literary lunches are massed with them. If one is too early one is given a whirl round the town and shown the sights and very interesting that can be. On one occasion I was taken to a coffee Klatch of ladies, where I was introduced to the Lady Mayoress, who greeted me with the words:

'Oh I'm so relieved it's you! I thought you were going to be a Chinese lady.'

I was a little startled by this until the secretary replied:

'No, Lady Mayoress, that's next month, when we have Ying Si-fong telling us about Flower Decoration. This is Mr Bull, who has come to talk to us about Teddy Bears.'

But soon it's time for lunch, which is usually pretty ropey (there have been notable exceptions like Newark but that was a notable visit throughout), and sharp at two o'clock I am on my feet. I am practically always introduced by

Madam Chairman who can be wildly disconcerting with remarks like:

'Did you *really* get the D.S.C.?' or 'You won't be *too* long will you, Mr Bull, because most of the ladies have their bridge at 3.30.' On one occasion I didn't like to say that I'd already set my sights on catching the 3.19 out of the city.

My lecture, as it's so flatteringly called, lasts about forty minutes, with five minutes for questions. Unlike most speakers I vary it a great deal according to the look of my audience, before I get to my feet. At the first yawn I tend to say something so outrageous or unexpected that those about to have a zizz pull themselves together, but I'm afraid most of them don't mind who talks to them, as long as they are talked *at*. If I can't hold them with Teddy Bears I switch to my Greek House or vice versa. But they are mostly pretty good, though I don't envy the secretaries who have to engage us and deal with complaints. I gather that speakers are criticized mainly for dress. 'She looked so dowdy, considering ...' or 'My dear, did you see? He had frayed cuffs.' I actually overheard the latter, just before I was about to get to my feet. They weren't talking about me but it did so happen that my zip had broken that morning so I wasn't exactly sitting or rather standing pretty. The speed with which I sat down and stood up must have surprised a good many of my audience. I resembled a rather plump Jack in the Box.

Once a year there is an excruciatingly droll ceremony at the Dorchester Hotel where we all pay a great deal for our lunches and meet our opposite numbers, the Secretaries and Madam Chairwomen, I mean Mesdames Chairwomen, bearing on their breasts the names of their club. Here they march round and give us (our names are clearly visible) the once over. And it's just that. I remember being slightly disconcerted last time when a couple of prospective employers came right up to me, studied my badge and one said to the other, 'Peter Bull', and the other said 'Yes, we *thought* of having him but we didn't.'

One drifts round as in a dream and every now and then some kinder ladies address one. Everything depends on how one impresses them at first sight and one can't help thinking of the old slave markets in New Orleans, though they don't actually handle one's privates to see if one is capable of great fertility. Perhaps it'd perk things up if they did. My godson, Sheridan Morley, had warned me of the embarrassment of the whole occasion as he's been part of the lecturing syndrome for some time. It was very reassuring to see him around.

Later one goes into lunch to a vast room which stretches for miles. At the centre table are all the big knobs of the Associated Speaking world, flanking Mr and Mrs Cyril Fletcher (Miss Betty Astell to you and me). The smaller fry are dispersed at various tables and I was fortunate enough to be at the table of the new double-barrelled secretary of the Jersey Luncheon Club, who didn't actually engage me on the spot but was plainly as nervous as I and equally bewildered. It was both our christenings in this particular battlefield. After a lunch of which I can remember little, except that there seemed to be a lot of peas, came the speeches. Mr Fletcher made a welcoming one, with wit and tact, and then the fun began. Lady Barnett thanked Mr Fletcher on behalf of the guests and both sides were asked to voice any complaints. A mild lady on behalf of the Clubs said it would be a help if speakers engaged and unable to fulfil the appointment could give plenty of warning. For the Speakers the Duke of Bedford got up and complained that there was far too much talk about local matters before he was allowed to speak. He implied that he had come to Speak and not listen to whose marrow had won the Women's Institute competition.

It was at this moment that I thought that all the secretaries and chairwomen who annually paid vast sums to hear His Grace Speak might rise in a body and string him up to a lamp-post outside the dear old Dorchester. However A. N. Other got up and said that he couldn't disagree more with the Duke and was delighted to hear all the local news and that was almost the nicest thing about travelling round lecturing. I could see thousands of pencils working overtime and I don't think A. N. Other need worry about his bread and butter, to say nothing of jam, for several seasons. A lady got up and said calmly and without malice and anger that she had had only one booking the whole season and wasn't it possible for anyone who wasn't a TV personality to interest the clubs. There was a lot of shuffling of feet at that. My godson relieved the tension by getting up to complain that it would be nice if he wasn't always greeted with the phrase, 'Oh you're much fatter than you look on the telly!' After him there was a good deal of waffling and I left the building fairly quietly. As I was getting my coat, Mr Harry Wheatcroft presented me with a red rose or three, which was the kindliest gesture of the whole occasion.

I don't think I shall go next year and maybe the novelty of the whole merry-go-round will have worn off by then. At the back of my mind I feel it's all a dress rehearsal for a lecture tour in America where the financial rewards are tremendous. My agent over there tells me that I can expect to get $850 per talk and a month of that per year would suit me fine. He is however trying to persuade me to make it a whole evening which worries me somewhat. He has suggested that I should include theatrical readings and heaven knows what else, so I suppose it's back to my long speech from *Luther* and dear old Sergeant Buzfuz. He has however suggested the ideal title for such a disastrous-seeming enterprise.

'An Evening of Bull.' Well we shall see, shan't we?

Envoi

OH, I do hope I've spelt it right! But I'm sure it's the chic way to wind up a volume of 'belles lettres' ('beautiful letters,' if you remember I kindly explained to you in the Foreword). The biggest dictionary to which I have access describes an 'envoi' as 'serving as a dedication or a similar postscript to a prose composition'. Fair enough, though, it also says it *can* mean 'A short story concluding a poem in certain archaic forms, such as a ballade'. Ballade all this farrago hasn't been, so let's settle for the first meaning.

What I find so exciting about life is the way that it takes hold of you, if you give it a chance, by the scruff of the neck and flings you up in the air or even sideways. Particularly the latter, if you are trying to cross Hyde Park Corner, without using one of those subterranean passages. In these there is bound to be a full orchestra of assorted hippies dotted around, stoned out of their minds but quite keen on the new p's which one throws at them out of sheer terror.

Now, if someone as late as 1969 had told me that within five years I would have bought a freehold building in the W.8 area and be the guest of honour at the annual Astrologers' Feast at the National Liberal Club (of course) I would have snorted 'Ha! Bloody Ha!' And if he had further hazarded a guess that I would more or less have opted out of the entertainment world, and taken to lecturing to Ladies in Hats the length and breadth of England, I would have laughed in their faces, nay howled. How funny 'nay' looks by the way, doesn't it? It's so rarely used nowadays that it looks embarrassed at suddenly being exposed. Now 'viz' never gives that impression. Bold as brass that one, and I tend to take it for a trot quite often.

Anyhow here I am embarking on a couple of new careers at the age of 60 (61 by the time this reaches W. H. Smythe and Son: I prefer the less common spelling of Smith myself). There are two factors which I think have contributed to my new lease of life. One was or were the words of wisdom given me by my kindly stockbroker. I mentioned that I was thinking of going into the Gipsy Tea Room business. He was visibly concerned by the hazards of such an undertaking and urged me to desist. He intimated that, if I was careful, I could easily retire on my capital. An occasional theatrical job would of course help.

I suddenly had the vision of one of those slightly florid gents you see in the ads, sitting in a pretty unsafe-looking deck chair in a garden full of hollyhocks. Far too near there is a lawn-mower and, though the turf looks in spiffing condition, there is no doubt that at any moment the wife is going to scream out of the kitchen window, 'Are you going to finish the lawn or aren't you?' And he'll have to rise, mount the bloody machine, and have a stroke. No, not for me.

The other factor in my change of life has been the appearance in it of Mr Howard Gottlieb, who looks after the Lugar Memorial Libraries at Boston University. Some years ago he contacted me in New York and, to my genuine astonishment, asked me if I would donate in my will all my papers and MSS to his establishment. I was so flattered that I said, 'Oh but yes, Mr Gottlieb' immediately, without thinking of the consequences. It wasn't till several years later that I realized how hair-raising the prospect is for whatever poor person has to sort out My Things. I suspect it will be Mr Busby. And I can't think having a book dedicated to himself will lessen the sweat and boredom of his task.

To begin with, I have kept every scrap of correspondence since I was about 18. It is contained in several trunks, cases, packing cases and cardboard boxes. The letters, postcards and memos are in no sort of order and included are love letters, hate dittos, demands for money, invitations to balls, first nights, tennis and frightfully few to marriage. They are in packets supposedly sustained by perishing rubber bands. Then there are cartloads of press-cuttings, not just quotes about my beautiful performances or embarrassing dittos, but whole cast lists of films and plays, which just mention my name. Reviews of my books and the entire Teddy Bear correspondence files, which fill a whole chest of drawers by themselves, are also sitting waiting for Mr Gottlieb.

But then what exactly does Mr G. define as 'My Papers'. Does he include in his calculations my collection of newspapers and magazines. If so, he is in for a bit of a shock because he will have to cart across the Atlantic whole sets of film and theatre magazines, dating back, in some cases, to the beginning of the century. No, he can't have *all* those, now that I come to think of it, as I left the most valuable of them to godchildren and friends in my will, before Mr Gottlieb came into my life.

So he'll have to content himself with the volumes of theatre counterfoils which I kept so assiduously in loose-leaf books for so many years to see if I ever sat in the same seat twice, though what good that information would have done me must remain a mystery. And he can have all the sexy magazines like *Screw*, *Pussy*, *Gay Power* and one copy of *Fuck*, which I'm afraid only had one issue as far as I know. There are also magazines as diverse as the *Messina Naval Base Magazine* and the *Chubby Chasers Gazette*, which was a rather specialized monthly devoted to persons who desired to meet those inclined to ample proportions and advertised their specifications and vice versa.

Old copies of *London Life* will flummox him a good deal, I fancy, though only because it was about forty years ahead of its time. Nowadays when all the newsagents' notice-boards are full of cards which say things like 'Air Hostess seeks Ground Position' or 'Strict ex-German mistress seeks apt pupils', *London Life* must seem a little tame but in the thirties it was sensational. The first few pages were entirely devoted to Society Gossip and the doings of 'Princess Lillibet' as Her Majesty the Queen seemed to be called in those days. But as you turned the pages, you were conscious that the photographs in the magazine were a trifle peculiar. They all featured ladies with long hair or wearing high boots, and the gents were tattooed, wearing ear-rings or ankle-length macs. In those days it came under the heading of Perversion with a capital P. Nowadays this sort of rig is *de rigueur*.

But *London Life* was considered very daring by Miss Hermione Gingold, Mr Robert Morley and me, with its correspondence columns full of contributions from such fascinating characters as 'Marquis of the Old Regime', 'Madam Pince-Nez' or quite simply 'Mac and Mud Mad'. I was fortunate enough to get hold of a series of bound volumes, which would now fetch huge sums at Sotheby's. In a fit of mad adoration I gave them to Miss Phyllis Robins on the first night of my penultimate theatrical enterprise as an entrepreneur. This was a musical version of Noel Langley's *Cage Me A Peacock*, on which I lost just 4000 quid, which included my Naval Gratuity. Miss Robins lost the copies of *London Life* in a fire. I don't know who was the biggest loser.

If only I had more actual MSS to leave lying about for Mr Gottlieb. I can't help wishing that I was or had been Anthony Trollope's mother. You see, she appeared to write best when her husband and at least two of her children were ill and being nursed by her. She kept house and supported the entire household on the royalties from her novels. I would have you know that she produced one hundred and fourteen volumes, of which the first was not written until she was fifty years of age. She managed also to change residence and re-establish herself and her family six times in ten years. Mr G. would have revelled in her, I'm sure.

Come to think of it, there is a third factor which has caused me to reconsider my way of remaining life, and that is my growing distaste for being a member of the profession with which I have flirted for nigh on forty years. I suppose I have never really been mad about acting *qua* acting: I've just liked being around mixing with the magic which is part of the theatre. Or was! It's no good people telling me that I'm just a dreary old philistine banging on about 'the good old days'. I am but I can still thrill when I see certain performances by Mr Scofield and any of the Knights and some of the Dames in a really worth-while play, preferably one which requires the curtain to go up and certainly come down. In under two and a half hours if possible.

But how I dread going to the theatre nowadays if it entails finding them already 'at it' as one gropes one's way to an expensive seat. Sometimes there are just four chairs on the stage or a lot of dying people in hospital beds (*The National Health*) or the inhabitants of a dosshouse scratching themselves for lice (*The Lower Depths*). In these circumstances I'd like to be warned and arrive at 7.29 for a 7.30 curtain. Not that there *would* be a curtain but then I know I'm unlikely to be entertained if there are no curtains except the one for our especial safety. For me the rise and fall of them has always symbolized excitement, anticipation and above all, mystery. If it is already up when one sits in one's seat, it is so easy to have the illusion of being at 'the theatre' shattered before the entertainment starts.

The outside world is so lacking in real glamour and laughs and I am bound to say I pay more attention to the phrase 'It's a lot of rubbish but very entertaining' than 'You *must* see it. It gives you a lot to think about.' When I go round talking to the Ladies in Hats, I see many a moist eye when I start talking about The Theatre in the Thirties. In 1933 as you strolled up Shaftesbury Avenue, you could see the

Lunts at the Lyric, Elisabeth Bergner (and incidentally me playing three parts and saying four lines at the Apollo), Ina Claire at the Globe, Marie Tempest at the Queen's, Fred Astaire (in person) at the Palace. And down the Haymarket Yvonne Printemps was at His Majesty's in *Conversation Piece*. And around the Strand Gladys Cooper and Sybil Thorndike were holding the fort. What happened to the heritage of the Great Leading Ladies of the theatre? Now the nearest approach we have to them is Mr Danny La Rue.

And that's enough of my personal dissatisfaction at the theatre in general. I would be hypocritical if I didn't admit that the main reason for my easing gradually out is that I suffer worse and worse from nerves as times goes on and I die a thousand deaths on first nights. Most actors do, of course, but my incipient ulcer and common sense whisper 'It ain't worth it, mate.' But and it's a huge *but* I am greatly disturbed by the current position and dignity of the actor. When I first went on the stage in the thirties there seemed a very personal relationship between managers, actors and agents and one had a feeling that there was a general, if spasmodic, interest in one's welfare. But now it's become such a jungle of a profession that it is literally everyone for himself.

With 70 per cent unemployment (at the current count) most actors will settle for any job which will prevent them from starving. It is arguably the only type of work where payment for services has decreased as the cost of living has risen. And hurriedly I want to say that I'm not belittling the splendid achievement of British Actors Equity Association in raising the minimum wage on all fronts. I have no doubt but that stage staffs, technicians and beginners are nowadays adequately recompensed, but for the old warhorses and those who have been accustomed to decent salaries and a complementary standard of living, it is humiliating to have the phrase 'Of course there's no money' hammered out at one, before one has even had the chance to decide whether one wants to do it or not. And it's a vicious circle.

The agent, who has also suffered greatly from the slump, dare not, except in exceptional circumstances, try his and/or his client's luck by insisting on the offer being raised and thereby possibly offending the prospective employer. So he advises his client to accept. Recently I was offered a small role in a big film at rather less than I was getting as a daily rate in the late forties. It wasn't a wildly interesting or attractive role and my agent had already used the phrase 'There's no money'. I turned down the part and the next day the director called and asked why I wasn't doing it. Even he was shaken by the reply, the money was trebled, and I accepted with alacrity.

Now I'm one of the lucky ones, in that I have a bit of private money, a few other projects going, and am not besotted about the acting. But most actors yearn to act all the time, therefore it is not quite the same thing as dockers who strike because they are not all that mad about docking. Ditto postmen, miners and electric gentlemen. But your average actor would rather be carrying on in a Soho basement at lunchtime in an absolutely incomprehensible play in return for expenses and a 'Wimpy' than not act at all.

The final straw, as far as I was concerned, was my treatment in the film of *Alice in Wonderland*. After Orson Welles, Robert Morley, Peter Ustinov and, it was rumoured, Peggy Mount had turned down the part of 'The Duchess', I was offered it. 'Of course there's no money' was relayed to me from my agent. Now there are practically no parts I really lust to play except possibly this particular one. I was offered it in the Jonathan Miller TV version and I played it in an earlier version of which I can remember little except that I had laryngitis which made my performance even more macabre than usual and Miles Malleson was breath-taking as the Mock Turtle. So I accepted the part in this version, though the salary was laughable. Thrown into the lump sum of £250 were rehearsals, recording sessions, post-synchronization and recording, of which more anon. It finally worked out at under £25 a day which didn't compare favourably with the three figures I have been fortunate enough to reach in the years of plenty.

But that is not the point. In fact I would have done this particular part for nothing as I rather fancy myself in it and I liked the original Lewis Carroll script as it had not been tampered with. It was just the 'There's no money' bit when a film company have secured the services of Sir Ralph Richardson, Sir Robert Helpmann, Peter Sellers, Spike Milligan, Michael Crawford, Dudley Moore, Dennis Price and Dame Flora Robson among others, to say nothing of John Barry to compose the numbers for the film. One couldn't help wondering if the producers said 'There's no money' to all that lot.

After I'd agreed to do the film, I was minding my own business in the shop when an American friend of mine came in suddenly out of the blue and bought a Virgo T-Shirt. I asked him what on earth he was doing here and he said, with a slightly evil smile, that he was over on a jaunt from the States with a lot of journalists to publicize *Alice in Wonderland*. As the film was nowhere near completed, this bit of information surprised me a bit. I asked him what paper he was representing and he said *Screw*, which is the notorious Number One pornographic magazine in the States. Even before making further enquiries, I speculated how the Mormons, who were backing the film, would react to paying vast sums to transport a member of the staff of this magazine to promote a classic not entirely associated with adults.

Then I heard the whole story from *The Village Voice*, a New York weekly whose representative had also joined the convoy. The Mormons had chartered a plane to bring 150 people over on a free, all-expenses-paid, five-day trip to London and filled it with, among others, the Mayor of Salt Lake City, the owner of the largest theatre chain in Hudson's Bay, a male junkie 'groupie' wearing a *Screw* T-shirt (oddly enough not my chum), 19 smiling Mormons, a huge white Bunny, a man from *American Girl*, a pregnant film reviewer from *Parents' Magazine*, 95 Movie House executives from Memphis, 11 bronzed and smiling P.R. representatives, a former all tabernacle basket ball player from Brigham Young and a very witty gent from *The Village Voice* to whose report I owe such invaluable information.

The whole project had apparently been planned in just over a week and the call went out from Salt Lake City to the harassed P.R.'s 'Fill us up a plane.' The next day telephones started ringing all over the country. 'Got somebody in your office wants to go to London?' 'Don't hang up, we'll find someone' was the unvarying reply. One of the radio stations found four, a hip FM magazine two and so did *Scholastic Magazine*. A *New York Times* syndicate celebrity reporter found that her husband, a free lance photographer, could be persuaded to go. Several mysterious 'secretaries' showed up. One guy wanted to look up his uncle, another had a girl friend in Paris or was it Prague? (*The Village Voice* asked.)

The plane left about midnight minus a representative from *Glamour*, who hadn't apparently realized until too late that one needed a passport to get into England from America. Directly across the aisle from *The Village Voice* there was a vast horde of middle-aged merry makers who constantly struggled up and down the aisle slapping other delegates on the back (or, if they were women, on the ass, *The Village Voice* delicately points out), making new friends at the tops of their lungs, swilling and spilling bourbon ('stupendous amounts of liquor set the cabin awash', quote unquote), goosing each other and telling dirty jokes. This apparently went on all night.

Instead of touching down at 10.20 a.m. on the Saturday, the BOAC machine clocked in around 1 p.m. Its contents were disgorged at the Skyway Hotel, which was handy for Heathrow but not for Shepperton Studios, where *Alice in W* was being filmed or indeed for the organized trips to theatres, Windsor Castle, Blenheim Palace and even St John's Church, Smith Square, where on the Tuesday the motley group was to assemble rather surprisingly for an English Afternoon Tea.

Round about this time I have to report that my agent and I were struggling to get me a tiny percentage from the sale of the L.P. of the music of the film on which I was singing two numbers. The producers thought it preposterous and at one moment it was obliquely threatened that my voice would be dubbed if I insisted on royalties. It was then that I went on strike. I just mentioned (this was the Wednesday) that in that case I wouldn't be turning up on the set on the Friday. This did work, I must say, but it didn't improve my relationship with M. René Dupont, an English gentleman in charge of the financial relationships between artistes and those acting for the Mormons. I must add that nice Will Sterling, the actual writer and director of the film, knew nothing of the goings-on and indeed was having struggles enough with the producers, without extra traumas.

In the meantime the denizens of the Skyway Hotel were having a high old time. A conservative estimate put the cost for each of them to complete the trip (drinks, meals, entertainments, etc.) at round about the same amount of money as I got for the entire film, for which the distinguished cast, as I have already pointed out, was solemnly assured that 'there was no money' for them.

I have just to report on the final phase of the Journalists' Junket, which consisted of a mass Elizabethan dinner at the Gore Hotel, where wenches in low-cut period costumes tend to call the gentlemen 'sires' and the ladies 'mistresses'. The meal is served on wooden plates, food is eaten with the fingers and you are allowed to spit on the floor (if the desire takes you). Scraps are meant to be left for the poor but if the Sires and Mistresses fail to leave them, the penalty is to tell a story. On this particular occasion (and I am indebted to *The Village Voice* for this particular juicy morsel of information): 'the tale-teller arose. He seemed perfectly average, middle-aged, balding, but it was obvious that he had hidden strengths which had led to his being chosen for this role.

'"Well," he began "this is a story about the man with the ugliest private in the world."

'A paralysing silence transfixed the room. The wenches mouths dropped two feet. The Mormons wriggled like little caught fish. The sires and mistresses gasped and even the P.R.'s lost their tans on the spot. The punchline of the story was a gesture. And since the story-teller was a small man and made the gesture down at the level where it should be made, only the people at his table could see it. They shrieked with hysterical laughter. "What happened? What'd he do?" everyone else whispered. The Mormons saw at once that fast action was necessary. And so suddenly 19 Mormons rose, and, as one man, began going through the motions of wringing out their privates right before our very eyes. It was a sight no Gentile has ever seen before, or ever will again. I will remember it till my dying day.

'Well that was the highpoint. After that it could only go downhill and I won't bore you by relating the details. We did eventually see some *Alice in Wonderland* rushes but discussing them would only spoil the story. I slept through most of it, anyway,' concludes Mr Ken Sobol of *The Village Voice*.

I played most of my role in the film in a blazing temper, which I think probably helped my performance as the Duchess. I certainly suffered less from nerves than usual. I didn't appear however as angry as the 11-month-old baby whom I had to nurse throughout the kitchen scene.

It was rumoured that the casting department had held auditions for babies who looked as if they might really turn into pigs, though the proud mothers were not aware of this specification. The winner screamed its way throughout the shooting, went purple in the face with rage and hatred of me and at one moment I thought had a seizure. I felt the tiny body stiffen, as if in rigor mortis, when I was waltzing it round the room singing 'Speak Roughly to Your Little Boy' at it.

But it survived somehow, though at one moment the suggestion was put to me that I should throw the poor little mite up in the air and catch it. I did draw the line at this, though the singularly complacent father looked on in pride throughout the proceedings and didn't seem remotely alarmed at his offspring's relentless exposure to the lights and the dangers surrounding its appearance in the film.

Miss Fiona Fullerton, who gave her Alice, was a remarkably self-possessed young lady, who rather threw me on our first encounter. Having been summoned to rehearsal of the scene and after going to the length of hiring a car for the trip, I asked her if she'd like to 'run the lines' of the scene.

'Run the lines,' exclaimed Miss F. 'Haven't looked at them yet.'

Later however she was to prove a tower of strength. She guided me through the song and dance I had to perform in the Garden Scene. This sequence included 'The Moral Song', which was mercifully cut out of the finished film but, thank heaven, appears on the L.P., the profits from which I'd fought so bitterly for a right to share in.

My other song 'Speak Roughly' does not appear on the record, which is inexplicable as I do actually sing it in the film. But the whole of *Alice in Wonderland* was far more inconsequential than anything Lewis Carroll ever thought of.

I would like to conclude the saga of my role in this macabre comedy by reporting that I had no sort of communication with the film company at any time after the film. I wasn't invited to the Royal Première, I was never approached by any of the publicity people during the making of the film and it was only my friend Theo Cowan who managed to arrange for me to slink into a press preview.

This sort of behaviour is why, sires and mistresses, I'm not quite so keen on the actor's part in the present day entertainment industry. I might add that the Merrick affair put me off the theatre for a bit. I am fully aware that I have chosen two extreme cases but I am sure I would still be happier talking to Ladies in Hats and sitting at the cash desk of the Astrological Emporium. Why, only yesterday, a bearded chap arrived on a bike and asked if the Moon was in Gemini and I was able to tell him that it was. There's glory for you!

Finally I have to report that I've reached the end of this book without the 'I' flying off and I mustn't press my luck.

Any day now I expect a green card with these words printed on it:

'Howard Gottlieb hopes you will have a Happy New Year.'

Thank you, Mr Gottlieb, I am sure I will.

PAXOS (GREECE)
CHELSEA (ENGLAND)
MORNINGSIDE HEIGHTS (AMERICA)
BED (ALL OVER THE PLACE)
1966–1972 (ON AND OFF)